THE ART OF SIGNIFICANT SELLING, MARKETING AND CLOSING MORE DEALS

… Because The Sale Doesn't Begin
Until The Customer Says 'No'

BY **DAN CLARK**, CSP, CPAE

NEW YORK TIMES BEST SELLING AUTHOR
HALL OF FAME SPEAKER

Published by:

IZZARD INK
PUBLISHING

OTHER BOOKS AVAILABLE BY DAN CLARK

The Art of Significance-Achieving The Level Beyond Success
(Audiobook Also Available)

The Art of Significance Study Guide Training Manual

The Art of Significant Relationships

The Art of Raising Significant Children

The Art of Significant Leadership and Talent Development

The Art of Significant Speaking and Storytelling – What I Learned
From Zig Ziglar That You Should Know

The Art Of Significant Coaching And Building A Winning Team

The Art of Significant Network Marketing
(Audiobook and Study Guide)

Chicken Soup for the College Soul

The Most Popular Stories By Dan Clark
In Chicken Soup For The Soul

Puppies for Sale (Illustrated Children's Storybook)

Clark's Children's Classics

Soul Food (The Complete Dan Clark Collection)

Puppies for Sale and Other Inspirational Tales

Dan Clark's Humor File – A Repository of Jokes and B.S. Tales

The Treasury of Dan Clark Quotes, Lyrics and Poems

The Ten Time-Tested Truths Of Significant Selling

1. Sales is 'the transference of trust'

2. 95% of our best, most loyal clients and highest revenue generating customers come from referrals and our network circle of influence

3. Only when you get the man/woman right, can the world be right. Attitude really is everything. When your attitude is right your abilities will always catch up

4. You become the average of the five people you associate with the most. Which means you must be willing to pay any price and travel any distance to associate with extraordinary human being

5. Wealth flows through you - not to you, which means you can get anything in life that you want when you are willing to help enough other people get what they want

6. You attract what you believe you deserve – in job satisfaction, level of income, and relationships at home, work and play

7. You must learn how to network at the highest levels and influence the affluent to build the size of your tribe of loyal followers who choose you, not just somebody who does what you do

8. Under pressure you don't step up your game. You succumb to the level of your preparation, training and practice. Which means pressure is not something that is naturally there. It's created when you question your own ability. When you know what you've been trained to do, there is never any question. That's why you train and practice so hard

9. It is not enough to say, 'I will do my best.' You must succeed in doing that which is necessary

10. The goal is to always have everybody leave you saying, 'I like me best when I'm with you, I want to see you again, and again, and…'

The Art Of Significant Selling, Marketing And Closing More Deals
… Because The Sale Doesn't Begin Until The Customer Says 'No'

ISBN: 9781630729288

TABLE OF CONTENTS

Acknowledgements

For my dad and mom who taught me through their example everybody is in the business of selling – and yet because no one likes to be sold and everybody loves to buy, selling is always about relationships built on total trust, integrity and a never ending commitment to service before self.

For my mentor and dear friend Zig Ziglar – the consummate salesman, regardless of whether he was selling motivation, his beloved Christianity, parenting skills or sales and closing techniques. He is greatly missed!

To my friends and mentors Royden Derrick, Gary Mangum, Blain Hope, Todd Peterson, Mark Victor Hansen, Jack Canfield, Berny Dohrmann, Simon Sinek, Rick Larsen, Todd Larsen, Walter Plumb, David Ayre, Sam Clark, Debbie Clark, Paul Clark, Brad Hatch and Doc Sansom for illuminating for me the Art of Selling.

For K.C., Danny, Nikola, McCall, and Alexandrea for finding wisdom, comfort, laughter, learning and solace in my speeches, stories, anecdotes, systems and words. I love you and need each of you in my life forever.

ENDORSEMENT FROM MENTOR ZIG ZIGLAR

"LET ME INTRODUCE and endorse my friend, Dan Clark. I met him in 1982, and sponsored him into the National Speakers Association, where in 1987 he became one of the youngest ever to earn his CSP – Certified Speaking Professional designation in the history of NSA. In the last 30 years, Dan has spoken an average of over 150 times a year to millions of people all over the world. He made the transition from educational learning institutions where he spoke primarily to high schools and teacher's meetings, into the business world. The neat thing is he gets repeat engagements. That really says something about the man. Interestingly enough, his versatility has taken him into some of the outstanding comedy clubs in America where he entertains and speaks. Dan is also a musician with considerable talent, having written a number of songs for some of the great talent in Nashville.

When you look at all of the things Dan Clark has done, you've got to be impressed. When you look at the man, you've got to be impressed. In fact, he will go down as one of the outstanding sales people of all time. In my judgment, maybe the greatest I've ever seen.

With all of this, Dan is a marvelous human being, one who practices what he preaches, one who has his life in balance, one whose family is extraordinarily important to him, one he is committed to bringing a message of hope and encouragement to any kind of audience he speaks to and/or for. Dan is one of the truly outstanding speakers in our world with a lot of good information that he delivers in an inspirational and humorous manner. He speaks and writes from his head and heart to your head and heart. Most importantly, he's a man of integrity. It's more than a cliché to say that what you see is what you get in Dan Clark. I encourage you to invite him to speak to your group. You'll be glad that you did."

—World Renown Motivational Teacher **Zig Ziglar**

MUST READ INTRODUCTION

"A lion doesn't concern itself with the opinion of a sheep."

LET'S FACE IT. As is the case in every profession and industry, one specific job/career is not for everybody. Because of our pre-disposition and inherent personality traits, some come easier than others. For example, I hate to do accounting, so I hire an educated, trained and competent accountant to do my books and file my taxes. I am not passionate about math or the slight bit interested in numbers. As a business owner I only want to know what the numbers are, not why and how the accountant tallied them.

However, my accountant actually gets excited at the end of every workday when the books balance! I am bored by the thought – he is thrilled at the result. Two different passions of two different people with different talents and inherent skill sets, who are striving to be the very best we can be in our individual chosen professions.

Sounds great, but the underlying challenge presented here that is always the 'elephant in the room' when we start talking about our professions, is the reality that most people do not get the same emotional satisfaction and adrenalin high from their jobs as I do as a professional speaker/author/leadership trainer, and that my accountant gets from crunching numbers. Bottom line? Search for your inherent talents – tap into your real passion – let go of your job/career and find your 'calling' that will inspire you to reach your ultimate capacity and potential as a human being.

As you do, perhaps becoming a Significant Sales and Marketing Professional is the answer and path you've been looking for? The good news is that everything required of you to start your own business and build it into the company you dream it to be is already inside of you. You need only read the right stuff and study the right program that will trigger enough passion, imagination, creativity and intestinal fortitude to let it out so you can use it to get from where you are to where you want to be! It really is this simple!

Personally I find motivation from the world of agriculture as it always illustrates the universal Law of the Harvest as it relates to increasing our personal and professional productivity. One of my favorite examples comes from 1948 to 2002, where the amount of farmable acreage in America did not increase. It remained the same for more than fifty years. However, the productivity and amount of crops harvested from those same acres increased by three and a half times during the same time period.

Bottom line. We cannot exceed potential, whether it be in land, resources, or ourselves. However, we can exceed expectations. By planting the seeds of higher expectations, the farmers brought forth an excessive harvest.

This reminds me of the lesson I learned as a house guest of three-time world heavyweight boxing champion Muhammad Ali, who taught me: "Impossible is just a big word thrown around by small men who find it easier to live in the world they've been given than to explore the power they have to change it. Impossible is not a fact. It's an opinion. Impossible is not a declaration. It's a dare. Impossible is temporary. Impossible is potential." Possible begins by dreaming the impossible dream!

Chapter One

The Art Of Becoming A Significant Sales And Marketing Professional

"Too many are living their lives 'hoping' to be happy, but because they only hope they never really are. They are waiting for someone to ask them to the Senior Prom and have never taken the time to learn how to dance."

—Dan Clark

Beholden to conventional wisdom, we don't put mental frameworks in place that allow us to understand significance and behaviors that produce it. As a result, lasting happiness eludes us, as do true individuality and real influence over others. The Art of Significance seeks to equip you emotionally and intellectually to take the higher road through life – and to feel more fulfilled in the process. Consequently, I have turned the word art into an acronym: Awareness of total truth (passionate inquisition), Refinement of character and values (continuous understanding), and the Transformational power of purpose (emotional application).

The intent of this book and presentation is to illuminate this reality, while continuously and subtly reminding you that at the end of every day and invisibly displayed on every business balance sheet is the truth: 'wealth flows through you, not to you – you can get anything in life that you want if you are willing to help enough other people get what they want.'

There are five required mindsets that not only serve as the foundation for becoming a Significant Sales and Marketing Professional, but when converted into daily thought and disciplined action, will transform your world of sales and marketing into an abundant life, living life unlimited, where you enjoy the benefits of Nutrition, Wellness and Health, Financial Freedom, an Active Lifestyle with quality and quantity family time, fueled by continuous Personal Development.

THE FIVE MINDSETS

1. HONOR TIME. CAREFULLY USE IT WITH URGENCY.

The currency of human beings is money. The currency of the universe is time. Money makes more money – time does not duplicate itself. You can't store time or put it off until another day. Your days are numbered and you will never get any more or any less. When your time is up, it's up. Consequently, do you ever stop long enough to wonder how much time you actually have left before you pass over to the other side? When will be your last day on earth? Are you ready, or will you have regrets? When was the last time you reflected on the fact that today is actually the first day of the rest of your life?

Today you've never been this old before, and today you'll never be this young again, so right now and every right now matters; no matter what your past has been you have a spotless future; you can't always control what happens, but you can always control what happens next. Do you really believe that one moment in time can and will change forever? I do. Proof?

I was once on a program with Henry Winkler – the "Fonz" from the old 1970's television sitcom Happy Days. Henry decided to take time off and treat himself to a matinee movie. To avoid having fans fuss over him, he entered the theater from the side door. As he sat down, a little girl in the row behind him smiled, pointed her finger, and slowly said, "Fonzie." Winkler snapped into the Fonzie character, flipping his hair, swiveling his hips, and glancing left and right. In his signature pose, he pointed his finger at the girl and said, "Hey! Whoa!"

To everyone's surprise, the lady sitting next to the little girl passed out. The theater manager came in to assist the woman who was now lying in the aisle and put a cold pack on her forehead. "Why did you pass out?" he asked.

Pointing to the little girl, she replied, "My daughter's autistic, and that is the very first word she has ever spoken in her entire life!"

It turns out the doctors had told this mother that her little angel would never be able to talk. But because of this mother's constant awareness of her higher purpose – making the best possible life for her daughter – she had gone the extra mile and taken her little girl to the finest therapists, hoping to help her at least understand the mechanics of speaking in case something clicked at some point in her life.

Think about this. If this mother had merely been patient, she likely would have fallen prey to insecurity and despair, welcoming the rationalization that we can do tomorrow what we should do today. She would never have endured to experience this wonderful moment of hearing her daughter finally speak.

2. Don't Let Your Past Define You.

I had a much less dramatic experience that happens every day at a Major League Baseball game that taught me this same message. In a nutshell, what we've been in the past does not make us who we are – what we've prepared ourselves to do in the future makes us who and what we are today. Proof?

I was watching the California Angels play the Kansas City Royals. Playing for the Royals was one of my greatest sports heroes, Bo Jackson. Because I'm such a huge baseball fan I always take a radio to the ballpark so I can tune into the sportscasters play by play and get the inside scoop on who is hurt, their batting averages, and which players are thriving and which are struggling. The game began and finally Bo Jackson's name was called as the next batter. As he strutted from the dugout toward home plate the sportscaster in my radio headphones explained that Bo was in a batting slump and had struck out the last nine times up to bat.

Think about this. If what we've done in the past defines us, then Bo would have stayed in the dugout whining, "Bo don't know! I'm not very good; I'm tired of failing and striking out – I quit." But because what we have done in the past does not make us who we are – what we have prepared ourselves to do in the future does, Bo Jackson confidently dug in, cocked his bat over his shoulder, and stared at the pitcher with his eyes daring the pitcher to throw him a strike. And do you know what happened? On the first pitch Bo swung like he meant it, and hit that ball over 500 feet as it sailed over the fence for a home run and continued skyward out of the entire park! The records show it was the longest home run in the history of the Angels stadium!

On a more personal note, Bo didn't just randomly swing at any pitch. He simply wanted to W.I.N., which means he focused on What's Important Now. Why? Because right 'now' is all we can control. Sounds elementary, but it is actually the profound secret to the solution to everyone's most pressing and depressing issue, 'Work/Life' balance.

Work/Life Balance

In the context of society's interpretation of time, work/life balance has been presented as an 'either/or' proposition, which creates guilt and an unsolvable crisis where if we spend more time at work to get a raise and a promotion our family time diminishes and our relationships suffer. But if we spend more time at home our professional opportunities for progress and development pass us by.

For this reason, we must learn to think like an all-star baseball batter, as Bo Jackson blocked out every distraction and focused only on one thing – the most important thing at that moment – seeing and hitting the ball.

Bottom line. Don't try to be a 'multi-tasker.' Become an expert 'juggler' – do what every champion juggler does. A juggler only controls the one ball in her hand. Once she has let go of the ball she has relinquished control – so why worry about it? And when it comes time to catch that ball again (as it once again re-emerges as What's Important Now), she again blocks out all distractions and focuses on catching the ball and doing what she needs to do until she lets go of it again to catch the next most important ball (and do the next most important thing – i.e. giving intense attention to a child, specific job task, spouse, coworker, school work, spiritual calling, civic duty, charitable giving, etc.) in that particular moment in time. Remember: time never stops, either should you, which means the best is always yet to be!

3. Become An Artist Of Significance – Achieving The Level Beyond Success.

To comprehend the difference between a successful person who gets what he thinks he wants at the moment based on the influences outside of himself, and a significant individual who wants what he gets based on the influences inside of himself, ponder the following:

To attract the right person we must first be the right person who makes our special someone feel more important than our work, our friends, or our hobbies, which requires time and attention and the realization that quantity is a quality in and of itself. In other words, you could spend your whole life with the wrong person, pursuing counterfeit happiness, working at the wrong job that you think is a career, but is definitely not a 'calling,' worrying about the future, making your decisions based on fear, disguised as practicality, and never dare to ask the universe for it. Or you could pursue real happiness by focusing on the present, making decisions based on love, illuminated as possibility, and decide to be great.

Bottom line. 'You already know that you could fail at what you don't want, so you might as well take a chance at doing what you love.' Success is getting what you want and finding happiness on a superficial level. Success is achieving goals – without having much purpose behind those goals. Success is creating the life you want – but leaving no legacy and making no difference in the grand scheme of things.

Getting What You Want Versus Wanting What You Get

What I'm calling significance is a higher state of happiness and fulfillment beyond the merely successful. Attaining significance means becoming aware of your purpose and working hard to bring that out in the world. Things happen for a reason, but it's our human responsibility to determine what that reason is – what our purpose is. To the extent that we can come to grips with reality and actually want what we worked hard to get, not merely to get what we want, we open ourselves up to significance. Sadly, too many of us – in fact, almost all of us – give up what we want most in order to obtain the empty success we think we want at the moment.

In other words, in order to 'have' more you first must 'become' more. Significance is not something you pursue. What you pursue alludes you, like chasing butterflies. Significance is something you attract by the person you become. So regardless of what you have as a goal, instead of focusing on what you have to 'do' to achieve the goal, write down who you need to 'become' to achieve your goal! If you want to have greater intimacy in your relationships, who do you need to 'become' to have greater intimacy in your relationships? If you want to be a better leader for your company or community, who do you need to 'become' in order to achieve that goal? If you want to grow your business and triple your income, who do you need to 'become' to achieve the goal?

To be a significant sales professional we must understand that we live in a customer driven economy. Which means our competitive advantage does not come from doing more than our competition – it comes from being willing to do what our competition is not willing to do. It is not enough to dazzle our customers, and 'create customer delight.' We must 'amaze' our customers by always giving more than we take!

Significant Individuals

Significance is the difference between your average physician, who has succeeded academically and graduated from a recognized medical school, and that rare doctor who travels to a developing country and performs cleft lip/ cleft palate surgery on children, seeking no money, recognition, or glory. It's the difference between NBA superstars Allen Iverson and Antoine Walker, who reportedly made over $100 million each in their basketball careers yet are now flat broke, and Magic Johnson, who promotes AIDS awareness and builds movie theaters, restaurants, and shopping malls in depressed neighborhoods, creating jobs and pursuing economic development for the disadvantaged and underserved youth.

Better still, it's the difference between the recording-industry pop stars and Hollywood celebrities with no education who think mansions, cars, and jewelry make them somebody, and my friend and colleague Kareem Abdul-Jabbar, the NBA's all- time leading scorer, who won six world championships and a record six regular season MVP Awards yet says his most significant asset is his mind. Since his retirement, Kareem has become a New York Times best selling author, filmmaker, and inspirational speaker. In 2011 the Obama administration appointed him the U. S. Global Cultural Ambassador. Even more significant, four of Kareem's five children have graduated from college, and his son, Amir, speaks three languages and graduated from medical school in 2012.

On a personal note, the difference between success and significance is a motivational speaker who is all about himself – writing, polishing, and presenting a speech that impresses the audience – and one who seeks to bless, not impress, inspiring the audience to become more of who they already are. Many people are successful but only a few are significant. Which would you rather be?

Becoming significant isn't about forgoing mundane dreams of success. It's about homing in on that deeper thing that matters to you, pursuing it, bringing benefit to others, and along the way, also achieving success for yourself, albeit perhaps in a different guise than you might originally have imagined it. Which company will achieve more conventional success – the success-oriented one whose employees, when asked what they do for a living, describe the task they perform every day, or the significant one whose employees energetically describe the purpose of the greater enterprise? Where will you find the elements that fuel sustainable business results, such as a greater sense of pride and loyalty, or the desire to increase productivity and profitability?

Remember:

*The most significant individuals I know are those
artists whose medium is life itself; the ones who*

express the inexpressible without brush, hammer, clay or guitar. They neither paint nor sculpt. Their medium is being. Whatever their presence touches has increased life. They see and they don't have to draw – they are the artists of being fully alive.

4. THINK LIKE A SONGWRITER.

In the world of music there are just twelve notes. Every song written in any language in any genre has been written with these same twelve notes. On a piano you can see the seven white keys and the five black keys, which constitute an octave that repeats itself along the eighty-eight keys of a keyboard. The only difference between one song and another is the order in which the twelve notes fall and the timing between them. And if you write a song in English, you use only twenty-six letters.

So what is the difference between a hit songwriter and a lousy songwriter? They have access to the same twelve notes and twenty-six letters. What's the difference between a significant banker and a successful banker? They have access to the same interest rates and the same economy. What's the difference between seven-figure income earning National Sales Champion who always exceeds his/her quotas and growth numbers, and an average wannabe who gives it mediocre effort to produce minimum requirement results?

The answer is the same for every aspect of our lives: passion, imagination, and creativity. It's what we do with the twelve notes and the twenty-six letters that's important, and why, when, and how we become brilliant at the basics that brings success and significance to our lives. In other words, it's not what happens to us that makes or breaks us. It's what we do with what happens to us that defines who we are. Remember, nothing happens to us. All things happen for us and give us experience. That means everything happens for a reason, but it is our responsibility to determine what the reason is.

Significant individuals achieve harmony through a perfect blend of passionate love, imaginative work, and creative service. Unless we consistently create opportunities to accomplish things we find important and meaningful, working to become better organized and balanced will serve only to fill up our time – and make us more frustrated.

PASSION, IMAGINATION, CREATIVITY

In music and in life, harmony remains an ineffable, almost magical experience, and that's because it brings together three things simultaneously: passion, imagination, and creativity. When we concentrate all of our being in the moment to achieve significance, these three things combined are what we project.

If you have *Passion*, you don't just hear, you listen; you don't just have sex, you make love; you don't just touch, you feel; you don't just play an instrument, you become the instrument and perform. You laugh longer, cry harder, connect deeper.

Passion is an internal drive to always do what is expected and then a little more – to feel absolutely everything you can possibly feel, to be fully alive. Passion amounts to heart – not what we do, but why and how we do it.

Imagination is visualizing, thinking, having curiosity and childlike wonderment, seeing more than others see, reading between the lines, having insight (not just eyesight), and going beyond the map, just as Christopher Columbus did in 1492. Imagination is mind over matter. It's not changing what is but improving it, making it more of what it already is.

Clearly, seeing isn't believing; rather, believing is seeing. Imagination is our ability to see the complete and comprehensive potential in ourselves and in each opportunity by always looking at life from an 90,000-foot perspective. And no, it is not limited only to seeing pictures in the mind. We can imagine a sound, taste, smell, physical sensation, feeling, or emotion. Training ourselves to readily use our imagination gives us the ability to combine all the senses, preview life's coming attractions, and embrace the observation that those who dream by day are cognizant of many things, which escape those who dream only by night.

Creativity is our ability to use the tools of any endeavor in new and appropriate ways. When we apply creativity, we arrange the stuff of our imagination into something that makes sense and works; we connect passion to heart and mind and take them all together to a place they cannot go by themselves. Thomas Edison had passion and imagination and continually rearranged what he produced as he pursued his goal of creating one awesome invention after another. By experimenting with thousands of possibilities, as the old but relevant tale is told, Edison failed more than most even tried and eventually failed his way to success.

Bottom line. If you continue to live in the past, your life will be history. Create your present and your future from your future. When Edison invented the light bulb, he didn't start by trying to improve the candle." Remember, no matter how many hit songs you have written; no matter how much of your company's amazing product you have sold in the past; and no matter how many wonderful people you have recruited into your Direct Sales business thus far, today and every new day is a new opportunity to take the same basic naked boring twelve notes and twenty-six letters, and with passion, imagination and creativity, arrange them into another beautiful 'hit' song/sale/ professional team member that allows you to continue to live a life of success and significance!

5. SET SIGNIFICANT EXPECTATIONS SO REJECTION BECOMES REFINEMENT.

In the world of music, every songwriter dreams and works hard to have a Platinum selling song. Every recording artist dreams and works hard to have a Platinum selling record. And because this is such an important milestone in their careers, the temptation to 'sell out' to accomplish this goal is always lurking in the shadows of the music industry. So what keeps songwriters and recording artists motivated to stay true to themselves and continually write their own songs and record their own choice of music? It's the reality that there are 300 million people in America. They can literally tick off and offend 299 million and still go Platinum! Ha!!

Moral to the story? Don't 'sell out!' Remember that the profession of selling is not for everybody. So don't let rejection hold you back or get you down. And definitely don't let what you cannot do interfere with what you can do!

ROGER CRAWFORD

Roger Crawford is a dear friend of mine and so is a tennis coach who stretched and helped him not only become successful, but eventually turn his life into significance. Consequently, I have a first hand account of the following story from both sides of the experience.

Roger was born into the world with serious birth defects, having only one finger on his right hand, two fingers on his left hand, no left leg and only two toes on his right foot. Growing up, everybody stared at him, made fun of his deformities, seldom invited him to play, and never invited him to parties. As a prisoner in his own body Roger became a recluse, feeling sorry for him self and never believing he had the power to change his predicament.

At least not until he met Tony Fisher. Tony was the tennis coach at San Jose State University in California, and one day in the middle of practice, up walked a nine year old boy who curiously stood at the fence for thirty minutes, quietly watching the workout.

Finally Tony noticed him and immediately walked over to talk. "Do you think you would like to learn to play tennis," Tony asked. "Holding up his hands Roger replied, "I can't." In a move of total class and full acceptance Tony replied, "What do you mean you can't? We can't afford to let what we cannot do interfere with what we can do!"

Call it what you will, but that same week the Wilson Sporting Goods Company had just released their new revolutionary metal tennis racket that consisted of a metal head with two metal shafts going down each side, merging into the handle and grip. Tony yelled to one of his players to bring their metal racket over to show Roger. Tony smiled and confidently explained that he had a plan.

Pulling out some tape Tony asked if he could wrap Rogers one finger on his right hand. Roger agreed. Tony then gently crammed Rogers taped finger into the space between the two metal shafts and took his left hand and taught Roger how to turn every shot into a two-handed stroke. Roger grew in confidence and skill and eventually tried out for his high school tennis team.

Not only did Roger make his high school team, he ended up playing in the Number #1 spot his senior year and ended up getting a full ride scholarship to the University of Loyola Marymount, in Los Angeles. Roger's tennis game became legendary, as his win/loss record in college was 46 wins and only seven losses. He beat Stanford's John McEnroe in straight sets! Truly remarkable!

But this isn't the story I want you to remember about Roger Crawford and his developed ability to accept himself, which invited and almost forced others to also accept him. After his incredible and inspiring success on the tennis team, Roger went to his parents and announced that he was trying out for the football team. Always supportive, but in this case reluctantly afraid, they encouraged Roger to counsel with the coach.

The coach could have backed down and talked him out of it, but instead told Roger that he was welcome as long as he didn't expect any soft and special treatment, and that he would have to work hard every day, participate in every drill, figure out how to lift weights, and never miss a practice. Roger was elated and committed right then and there to work harder than anyone else on the team!

Because Roger inspired every other guy on the team, the coaching staff decided at the beginning of the season to let him play an entire quarter of a game. Wouldn't you know it? They waited until the last game of the season to put him in! As Roger trotted out on the field to begin the fourth quarter, his fans began to cheer as he smiled and showed off his brand new uniform with knee high socks pulled up and his shiny cleats reflecting the sun.

Because his coaches were afraid that he would get hurt, they put him at the wide receiver position, which meant he took his place on the other team's side of the field spread out from his teammates. When the opposing team's fans saw him they started to laugh and make fun of him. When their coach noticed his hands he yelled loudly enough for the fans to hear, "Check him out. We don't even have to guard him!" So he took the player who was over Roger and moved him to the middle of the field to try and tackle the quarterback for a loss.

Sure enough, as Roger's quarterback barked out the signals and the ball was hiked, Roger did what he was supposed to do and ran down the sideline as if he would catch a pass. As the quarterback dropped back he immediately met the player who had broken through the line. In desperation and running for his life, the quarterback looked up to see who he could throw the ball to. Whom did he see? Roger running down the field with no one around.

While falling down, the quarterback let loose of a high, wobbly, wounded duck pass that was so high, Roger had a chance to spit on his hands for better grip and actually turn to see the guys who had stopped in their tracks and turned around to watch him. With his adrenalin pumping Roger caught the ball and continued running as fast as he could go toward the end zone.

As Roger passed the 50-yard line an opposing player started to gain on him. At the 40 the guy was only 20 yards behind. At the 20 the guy was only 10 yards behind. At the 10 the guy dove to tackle Roger, but was only able to grab his left leg. Roger jolted forward trying to escape. The guy yanked back. Roger again jolted forward and again the guy yanked back. Suddenly Roger's leg came loose, leaving the guy laying on his belly while Roger hopped on one leg into the end zone and scored the go-ahead touchdown that would eventually be the game winner.

As Roger did an amazing "end zone dance" hopping and spinning around and spiking the ball behind his head, his teammates caught up, lifted him to their shoulders, and paraded him around the stadium as the hero he was! When asked if that was the coolest, most rewarding thing that had ever happened to him, Roger smirked and replied, "No. The most rewarding thing was when I looked back at the guy on the ground with my artificial leg in his hands, with big eyes and a look on his face that said, "Whoa, dude. I had no idea! I'm sooo sorry! But good on ya!!"

Chapter Two

The Art Of "Knowing" You

"Be you – the very best you can be – everything you were born to be. You'll make a lousy somebody else."

—Dan Clark

"The goal is not to do business with everybody who wants what you have. The goal is to do business only with those who believe what you believe – so they choose you, not just someone who does what you do."

—Simon Sinek

Every individual desiring to live a life of significance needs to fully comprehend the difference between success and significance. I see mine as akin to the process by which silver is cast into art. As a precious metal, the silver is heated up, but because each vat of the molten metal responds differently to the same temperature, the artist has but one technique to know when the liquid stands ready for pouring into a beautiful shape. Only when the artist can see his face reflecting back at him from the silver is it ready to be molded into something more.

Whenever I have felt the "heat" or have been put to a test to see what I am made of, only when I've looked myself square in the eyes, with the proverbial man in the mirror reflecting back at me, have I been ready to mold and shape the man I am into the something-more man that I needed to be. (This is very much like a midlife crisis is, when you realize you're not the person you thought you were going to be. Most men have their midlife crisis at forty. I had mine at twenty- two!)

My dad always encouraged me to be me – the very best me I could possibly be – everything I was born to be – because I would make a lousy somebody else! So I ask, 'Who are you – really? Not who are you pretending to be, or what the world has labeled you. When we strip away society's perceptions, packaging and trappings, masks, racial stereotypes and job description pigeonholes that you have allowed others to put you in or influenced to be, who are you – really?

To illustrate: Prior to me being introduced as the keynote speaker at a national convention in San Francisco, California, I was sitting on the front row of the grand ballroom next to a young lady who I could tell was a little nervous. I asked her name and why she was attending the meeting. She sweetly replied, "My name is Yolanda, and pointing to the gentleman who was at the podium addressing the crowd, she explained, "I am an administrative assistant to him – the CEO."

Just then the man concluded his remarks and Yolanda was invited up on stage to sing the National Anthem. As she sang the final notes and hit that last exciting high 'A,' the crowd went nuts, applauding louder than I'd ever heard – with tears in our eyes, chanting her name! For two minutes the crowd applauded her extraordinary performance that literally ignited a deeper level of patriotism and American pride in all of us that we had never felt before! Yolanda was as spectacular as Celine Dion; as magnificent as Beyoncé; as emotionally stirring as was Whitney Houston's unforgettable performance at the Super Bowl in Miami right after the terrorists attacked America on September 11.

So, how did I start my speech? I asked the audience, "Is Yolanda an administrative assistant who happens to be an extraordinary super star performing artist, or is Yolanda an extraordinary super star performing artist who happens to be an administrative assistant?

WE DON'T SEE THINGS AS THEY ARE – WE SEE THINGS AS WE ARE

If we look out the same window at the same lashing rainstorm and I say, 'horrible,' and you say, 'wonderful,' the weather did not change! How you see the world and our place in it is a choice you make every hour of every day. So why sabotage your chances to succeed and destroy your opportunities to be significant by focusing on the negative? If you are one who wonders if the glass is half empty or half full, you've missed the point! It's refillable! Thinking positively or thinking negatively doesn't fill up the glass – the pouring does. It's easier to act your way into positive thinking than to think your way into positive action. It's not the sugar that makes the tea sweet – it's the stirring, it's the process of taking action knowing 'self is not discovered – self is created.'

Many will hear a loved one or close friend encourage them to 'go find themselves.' And where do most people go 'find themselves?' Yep. Boulder Colorado! We could get on a bus today and travel to Boulder and when we arrived we would see people walking out in the bushes with backpacks on 'looking for themselves!' They think they can go to the forest and somehow encourage themselves to come out from behind that tree. They act like they can play 'hide and seek' with themselves and close their eyes, count to 50, and yell 'come out where ever you are!'

No. Your reality is created by a conscious choice to be who you want to be, based on who you think you are, what you think you deserve, and how you see yourself in that role.

PRACTICAL APPLICATION

The real life practical application of this happened when I consolidated my six offices into one. I decided I needed a woman to run my operation and my life. I interviewed all of the people who my friends and colleagues recommended, who were extremely qualified on their resumes, but there was no emotional connection that stirred my soul – at least not until I interviewed Laura Calchera. Two months after I hired her I recommended that we order her a personal business card that she could give to everyone she met as a proud representative of the company we were building together. She agreed but asked what her title was, as we had never talked about it before. I told her I didn't care, that she should just make one up that suits her personality and job responsibilities.

A few days later the box of beautifully designed cards was delivered. To my surprise yet with my total blessing her business card read, 'Laura Calchera – Supreme Commander.'

Isn't it time for you to 'go big or go home;' 'let go and let love' dictate your next move?

If you feel out of shape and see yourself in the mirror as a 'fat failure,' obviously this negative attitude will not create any change. But if you simply change your perspective from negative to positive and see yourself as someone who has been very successful at putting on weight, you will change, because you realize that you gained weight one pound at a time and can therefore, lose it one pound at a time!

Bottom line. You don't create your present and your future from your past. When Thomas Edison invented the light bulb by trying to improve the candle. What you've been in the past does not make you who you are – what you dream about and have prepared yourself to do in the future makes you who you are today! Especially if you are willing to see your current self and laugh if necessary about the changes you should probably make that will ensure your desired future.

No Matter What – Keep A Sense of Humor

Be honest – are you strong enough with an understanding of the difference between the person and the performance that you can actually laugh at yourself? If you recall, one major ingredient in my recovery from my football injury that left me both physically and emotionally paralyzed, was being able to laugh in the reality that failure is an event, not a person. My dear friend, colleague, and country comedian T. Bubba Bechtol agrees and reminds the world of this in his act. Bubba is six feet tall, weighs more than 300 pounds and is the self-proclaimed national president of "Bubbas of America."

At the beginning of his comedy show he always comes out on stage wearing a skimpy t-shirt that exposes his navel (he thinks it makes him look sexy like Shania Twain) and pointing to the best dressed man in the crowd states, "You think you're successful? I beat anorexia and I've got it into permanent remission – it ain't coming back!" As the shocked audience breaks into loud laughter, he then says, "I haven't always been this big. I went to the doctor and he put me on a dehydrated food diet for six months. Then one day I got caught in the rain! I gained 150 pounds in five minutes! It was awful!"

On a serious note, because he is overweight Bubba started having chest pains, and luckily I was performing with him one night when they hit him the hardest. Although it was a serious condition, because the doctor in the emergency room had a sense of humor, Bubba was not only able to relate to him, but he was more accepting of the doctors harsh recommendations, which for the first time in his life, scared and inspired Bubba enough to start taking better care of himself when he left. Bubba explained, "Cut me some slack doc – my weight is a medical problem." To which the doctor explained, "No. The only medical problem you suffer from is that your body retains too much chocolate fudge cake!" Bubba countered, "I'm in shape – round is a shape! C'mon Doc, obesity runs in my family." To which the doctor sternly replied, "No. No one runs in your family!"

Remember: only when you see yourself as you really are, why you are, and where you are in your current reality can you change why you are and improve where you are. Given the reality of death, what really matters is not how successful we've become, but whether we've made a difference and left our families, friends, coworkers, neighborhoods, and countries in better shape than we first encountered them.

Financial and professional success is impressive, but the significance we hold in the eyes of others is important. When you get down to it, "best" and "great" lack meaning; they're just relative terms whose definition depends on what we compare them against. What most of us don't ever do is learn how to think truly uncommon thoughts so we can do truly uncommon things. In other words, don't regret growing older. It is a privilege denied to many! Don't fear death. Fear that you never really lived at all. Don't live in the past – it makes you depressed. And don't live in the future – it makes you anxious. Live only in the present – it creates peace.

DO WHAT YOU LOVE
SO YOUR LIFE MATTERS

So, again I ask, who are you? Does actor/comedian Jim Carrey describe you when he describes his father?

"You could spend your whole life worrying about the future, but all there will ever be is what's happening here and the decisions we make in this moment, which are based in either love or fear. So many of us choose our path out of fear disguised as practicality. What we really want seems impossibly out of reach – ridiculous to expect. So we never dare to ask the universe for it. I'm saying I'm the proof that you can ask the universe for it.

My father could have been a great comedian but he didn't believe that was possible for him. So he made a conservative choice. Instead he got a safe job as an accountant. When I was 12 years old, he was let go from that safe job and our family had to do whatever we could to survive. I learned many great lessons from my father, not the least of which was that you could fail at what you don't want, so you might as well take a chance at doing what you love."

CHAPTER THREE

THE ART
OF "BEING" YOU

"When you put a hard to catch horse in the same field with an easy to catch horse, you usually end up with two hard to catch horses. When you put a sick child in the same room with a healthy child, you usually end up with two sick children. To be disciplined, healthy and significant you must associate with the disciplined, healthy and significant."

—Dan Clark

EVERYTHING IN LIFE is simple – not easy, but definitely uncomplicated when we perceive it to be. Fortunately I learned this at eighteen years of age from my first roommate in college. In fact, everything I needed to learn in college I learned outside of class! In seven days my roommate taught me that when it comes to becoming successful and eventually transforming it into 'significance,' we need only cut through the clutter of complexity and focus on the simple attitude, truths and behaviors that define who we have decided to be.

It was my freshman year at the university and as a scholarship athlete I had no choice of a roommate. Each of us was simply assigned to another player on the team who played our position. We were introduced in the coach's office, assigned a dorm room, and then informed that because we were the last ones to check in we were given the very last room available – an older corner room. Without a word we departed the office and started hiking up the hill to our new home away from home. And yes, I complained the entire fifteen minutes it took to walk to our dormitory.

Day One: When we entered the building I continued to moan all the way down the hall, "What a drag this is going to be, having the smallest room and being crammed together for the whole year!" However, when we opened the door we were surprised and delighted to see a huge, oak-trimmed suite with a two-window view.

My roommate finally spoke and quietly said, "Yep, the early bird gets the worm, but the second mouse always gets the cheese."

Obviously I laughed, which finally snapped me out of my self-absorbed world and open to him and his world.

He was a big, strong, soft-spoken cowboy, with boots, a big belt buckle, a huge smile, who obviously didn't speak much. As we chose our sides of the room and started to unpack our bags I asked, "What's your name?"

"Blain," he answered.

Five minutes of silence later I asked, "Where are you from?"

"Idaho."

Five minutes of silence later I asked, "Do you live in the city or the country?"

"Country."

Five minutes of silence later I asked, "What is your major?"

"Communications."

I laughed again!

Yes, Blain was a man of few words, but when he did speak, he was always deep and profound. In our first seven days together, Blain taught me everything I needed to know to be successful and become significant for the rest of my life.

Day Two: I had an old car with squeaky brakes. I asked Blain if he knew anything about cars, and could he repair what was wrong. That afternoon he jacked up my car and took off a wheel. He quickly checked it and put it back on. He then opened the hood and fiddled around for a minute. Dumbfounded, I asked him what he was doing? He simply replied, "I couldn't fix your brakes, so I just made your horn louder!"

Day Three: We had the first class of the day together. It was Introduction to Marketing. The professor said, "Take thirty minutes and write an ad. Use as many words as necessary, but keep it to one page." After a while the professor called on three different people to share. They read full-page, wordy essays. The professor then called on Blain. He quietly read, "For sale: Parachute, only used once, never opened, small stain."

We laughed. The professor was intrigued and inquired if he had any other thoughts he would like to share. Blain quietly drawled as we all held our breath, "Statistics prove that most people have serious accidents within five miles of their home. So call me as your realtor, and I'll help you move!"

We all burst into belly-shaking hoots and cheers!

Day Four: The sociology professor ironically didn't seem to care about anything or anyone. He didn't call the roll and only talked for one minute at the beginning of class to tell us what chapters to read. Then he sat down, put his feet up on a table, and read a magazine for the next thirty minutes. I commented to Blain, "How can he teach us when he is not even involved in the class?"

"He can't," Blain replied. "You can't farm from the city."

I then asked him if he were the professor, what would he teach? Blain replied, "Ninety percent of success is half mental."

I laughed and asked, "What?"

With a serious face, Blain explained: "Yep. Success is 10 percent inspiration and 90 percent perspiration – 10 percent what happens to you and 90 percent what you do with what happens to you. The half mental is attitude and the other half is action."

Hmmm. Not so off-the-wall after all.

Day Five: Already, some of the guys in our dorm who had arrived as high achievers with high moral standards and high athletic and education goals, had succumb to the influences of the average, let their guards down and decided to take the 'path of least resistance.' When I asked Blain his opinion he picked up his notepad and said, "Funny you ask. I had to write three short poems in my English class today that pretty much explain what's goin' on with these fellas:

'On top of old Smokey all covered with snow, I lost my best bird dog by aiming too low.'

'It's better to shoot for the stars and miss than to aim for a pile of manure and hit!'

> With garbage and junk our big can is well fed,
> This trash we don't want we can burn it instead.
> But what about dirt that you've heard or you've said,
> Oh what can be done with a garbage can head?

Day Six: It was the weekend, and I asked Blain if he wanted to go to a party. We went. Within fifteen minutes the fraternity boys tried to pressure him with the usual, "C'mon. Chill out. Loosen up. Smoke a little dope, drink a few shots, get down tonight." I asked him if he wanted to leave. Blain answered, "No. But you shouldn't try to teach a pig to sing. It's a waste of your time, and it annoys the pig! And when you hang around with these type of folk you gotta remember two things: 'If you ain't the lead dog the view don't change much,' so you shouldn't follow them knowing you never drink down stream from the herd!"

Again I was stunned into 'hmmm.'

Day Seven: I was tired and wanted to sleep in. But Blain was up bright and early. I asked him where he was going all dressed up. He said, "Church." Sarcastically I poked fun. "Why would you go to church? Your parents aren't here to make you."

Blain put me in my place with his answer: "It's what you do when the coach is not around that makes you a champion. The Native American Indians say, 'Short alive, long time dead.' We shouldn't just learn and do things that will help us while we're alive; we should learn and do things that will help us when we're dead! You should come to church with me."

I defiantly demanded, "Give me one good reason why I should."

Blain pretty much summed up the week when he confidently said, "I'll give you five reasons why, beginning with this 'Priority Guide' that my mama sent with me to hang on my mirror as a reminder to always be the real happy me:

Make A List Of Things That Make You Happy
Make A List Of Things You Do Everyday
Compare The Lists
Adjust Accordingly

"It's better to build a fence at the edge of the cliff
than to park an ambulance at its base!"

"It's better to prepare and prevent
than to repair and repent."

"Hope is not a method and faith
without works is not faith at all."

"Sorry isn't a verb. Don't expect it
to fix things for you."

In seven days and in about seven minutes total, I learned never say never, you can only do what you can do, less is more, you must be present to win, choose your influences, be true to your values and yourself, and prevention is always better than rehabilitation – common sense truths that remain right and true regardless of taste, opinion, age, sex, race, belief, language, culture, political party or country. Right has always been right, or we can't call it right. And yes, 'Be You – you'll make a lousy somebody else!'

CHAPTER FOUR

THE ART OF FINDING YOUR PERSONAL 'WHY'

"The two most important days in your life are the day you are born and the day you find out why."

—Mark Twain

DAN'S 'SIGNATURE' STORY

I HAD NO reason to believe the words of Nietzsche, "If you know the 'why' for doing, you can endure almost any 'how.'" At least not until I had a life changing significant emotional event that illuminated: when you know why you are doing something, when the hard times come, and the disappointments overwhelm you, and rejections start weighing you down, your reasons will be your rod and staff to comfort you and pick you up and remind you what my friend and colleague Les Brown says, 'When life knocks you down, do everything you can to land on your back, because if you can look up you can get up!' I now know it's our reasons that get us back on our feet!

For your reference and as I documented in my book "The Art of Significant Leadership and Talent Development, I played American football for thirteen years, and was a projected #1 Draft choice into the National Football League by the Oakland Raiders. On the first day of practice in my last season, when my lifelong dream of playing both professional football and baseball were alive and well, we were running a tackling drill where two of us ran into each other at full speed. From fifteen yards apart my teammate's helmet violently crashed into my helmet, my right shoulder was smashed into the cutting edge of my fiberglass pads, and we slammed to the ground momentarily knocking me unconscious. When Lyle got off of me my eye drooped, my speech was slurred, my right side was pierced with the penetrating pain that felt like my body was on fire, and my right arm dangled helplessly at my side.

I remained numb for fourteen months and went to sixteen doctors, fifteen of whom projected that my arm would always dangle at my side, telling me I would never get any better.

HAVE YOU EVER HEARD THIS? WHAT HAPPENS IF YOU BELIEVE IT? YOU NEVER GET ANY BETTER.

Sure it was a physical injury, but it effected my whole life. I was an athlete and got a lot of attention because of it. I was somebody because I played football and baseball and enjoyed free food at restaurants, status at celebrity galas, fame and glory. I was going to be an overpaid NFL superstar. But in a single moment, a freak accident took away my identity. Suddenly I was nobody to my coaches and nobody to my teammates and fans. Even more devastating, I became nobody to myself.

Have you ever lost your identify or at some point seriously questioned who you really are? Before you can like or love someone else, you first must like and love yourself. To like and love requires that you know and understand. I was lost, lonely, and confused.

I couldn't write – I was right-handed. I couldn't concentrate on work or education because it constantly felt like some wild animal was biting my neck and shoulder. I used to get electrical, shocking nerve impulses in my shoulder that would shake my arm like it was plugged into a light socket. This made me afraid to go out in public, especially on a date, because my arm might blast her in the chops.

One time I was sitting with my family at dinner when my arm flipped out and knocked a bowl of mayonnaise off the table. The next morning my younger brother showed up to breakfast wearing goggles and a batting helmet! Needless to say I hit rock bottom, and life as I knew it was nowhere to be found. I didn't know if I even wanted to live. Have you ever felt like that? Have you ever been so down and confused that you thought you should leave your family, isolate yourself from friends, and contemplate checking-out altogether? Before long I fell into what I thought was deep depression.

Why Would I Want To Give Up And Quit Everything?

The first reason I gave up and decided to quit was because I had confused who I was with what I did. Have any of you? I thought being an athlete was who I was, when in reality it was only what I did. Have any of you ever confused the difference between the person and the performance? Turns out that playing football and baseball was what I did, not who I was as a man. And when we identify ourselves in terms of what we do instead of who we are, we become human doings instead of human beings – unacceptable if lasting happiness and a life of significance is truly what we seek.

Sounds good and simple, right? However, shifting my priorities was the hardest thing I've ever had to do! In one moment, I was faced with the emotional pain of giving up my life's dream and the identity I had grown up with. Outside, I was an athlete. Inside, I knew it was time to find a new game.

The second reason I gave up and decided to quit was because I thought I was depressed. Which meant I was not just paralyzed physically – I was also paralyzed emotionally! And what happens when you think you are depressed? You are depressed.

However, through my experience I also know getting better mentally and emotionally was a prerequisite to recovering physically, and my improvement began when I realized there is a huge difference between being depressed and being disappointed – a giant difference between being depressed and being discouraged. And when you are disappointed and discouraged you don't need medication that flat lines your emotions and dries out your human spirit to fight and survive!

Psychologists remind us to be on guard of H.A.L.T.S. – which is avoiding being Hungry, Angry, Lonely, Tired and Sad – all of which distort our ability to think clearly and drain our energy to stay motivated.

When I was injured I didn't suddenly have a chemical imbalance and need medication. What I needed was a change in attitude and perspective to focus on identifying my why so I could again make winning personal!

Yes, I had some caring loved ones and associates come up to me and say, "I'm sorry and know what you are going through." But no they did not! No one does. Psychologists teach us that the average person talks between 100 and 200 words per minute, and yet we think between 200 and 400 words per minute – which means no one ever really knows everything we think or feel or want to say. The author Thoreau wrote, "Men lead lives of quiet desperation."

So what do we do? To whom do we turn? Luckily, I had some loyal friends and family members who stuck by me who continuously reminded me, "You can't quit – it's a league rule;" "No matter what your past has been you have a spotless future;" "We can't always control what happens, but we can always control what happens next!"

What I needed to begin my recovery was to start dreaming again and set some realistic goals that would keep me from letting what I could not do, interfere with what I still could do.

The third reason I stayed paralyzed for fourteen months was because I was asking the wrong questions. I was asking the doctors, "How to get better?" when I should have been asking myself, "Why should I get better?" You see, once we answer and identify "why," figuring out the "how-to" is simple. Not easy. If it were easy everybody would do it. Learning to do hard things is what makes life significant, and is what turns a boy into a man and a girl into a woman, and a manager into a leader.

TWO KINDS OF EXPECTATIONS

In order to always begin with the "why" in mind, you must understand there are two kinds of expectations: internal and external. Internal expectations are set for yourself by yourself. External expectations come from an outside source. Only when internal expectations match external expectations can you reach peak performance and create significance.

Internal low expectations are prevalent in our society as employees take long breaks and lunches, people cheat on their taxes and billing hours, educators take off sick days when they're fine, and way too many use the word "can't" when they really mean "won't." Guaranteed if they worked for themselves, they wouldn't be rationalizing their way out of integrity-based peak performance as seekers of mere instant gratification with no long-term vision.

When we associate with people with low self-esteem and low goals, over time we soften our desire to follow good reason.

Therefore, let us never underestimate the power of the mind and our power of intentions, as we usually rise to the exact level that we think we can. In the Olympic Games, time and time again when skiers, skaters, weightlifters, gymnasts, sprinters, throwers, or swimmers need to reach an exact score or time to win, they achieve the exact numbers on the scoreboard previously conceived in their minds and set as expectations by their coaches and the competition. Never higher, seldom lower, but exactly to the half-second, millimeter, or pound. When we engage both sides of our brain, somehow we always rise to our level of expectations.

Why didn't I quit?

"The greatest mistake you can make in life is to
continually fear you will make one.
When you are no longer able to change a
situation, it's time to change yourself and move
forward – because the best way out of fear is
through it."

My why became bigger than my 'why not.' In addition to my small group of true friends who kept me laughing and never allowed my to feel sorry for myself, there were three people who through a combination of outside-in inspiration and inside-out resolve, helped keep me focused for another six months of rehab, pushing me to relentlessly work hard and persevere until I recovered.

The person who kept me focusing on purposes instead of only setting goals was Vice President Normand Gibbons of the University of Utah, who in my despair gave me a recording of a speech given by internationally renowned motivational teacher named Zig Ziglar, who soon would become a personal friend and my sponsor into the National Speakers Association in 1982. I had never heard of him and thought his mom had run out of names!"

Out of curiosity I listened to his forty-five-minute speech, which through the use of humor and inspirational stories kick started my inside-out recovery. In his rhythmic southern drawl, Zig spoke directly to me through one specific story:

"A struggling oilman in Texas, in his last ditch effort to strike it rich, drilled one more time and hit a giant oil reserve so big that it gushed from the ground with such force that it literally destroyed the derrick. In an instant, the man became a millionaire. Or did he? Had not the oil always been down there? He had always been a millionaire but just didn't know it? All he had to do was dig down deeper and get out what was already there and use it for what it was meant to be used."

Can you see why this one tale meant so much to me? It pierced my mind and heart to look inside myself and hang tough long enough to drill down deep enough to discover the untapped reserve of passion, purpose, and perseverance that was stuck beneath my surface just waiting to be used.

I started getting better physically and emotionally only when I started focusing on purposes instead of just setting goals. I stopped focusing on having fame and started focusing on being whole. I discovered that in order to get a better answer you've got to ask a better question, and as I previously mentioned: the question I asked of each of the sixteen doctors —"How do I get better?"— was not the right question. The better question was not to the doctors, but to myself: "Why get better?" which generated a conclusion that: "Whatever it takes, I will endure to the end because this is what I am going to do when I get better."

Focusing on how to get better had set me up for failure because each doctor had a different theory, and the pain was so excruciating that quitting before fully recovering would have been easy and reasonable.

However, because of the influences I've shared and the emotional healing I first experienced, I fought back physically, mentally, and spiritually to a 95 percent recovery.

My conclusion? This football injury is clearly one of the best things that has ever happened to me. Don't misunderstand. My paralyzing accident isn't one of the best things that has happened to me – but what I learned about life and priorities and who I have become as a man as a result of going through this setback, makes it one of the best things that has ever happened to me. I now know that when you identify your 'why' and it becomes bigger than your 'why not,' you make winning personal and definitely discover 'how' to turn every stumbling block into a stepping stone, and every setback into a comeback!

Chapter Five

The Art Of Resetting Your 'Expectation Thermostat'

"Everybody is a genius. But if you judge a fish by its ability to climb a tree, it will live its whole life believing that it is stupid."

—Albert Einstein

WE ALL KNOW you can't coach results – you can only coach behavior. For this reason, regardless of what Covey suggested in his book, Seven Habits Of Highly Effective People," we cannot 'Begin With The End In Mind.' It creates a 'limiting belief' where you focus on a destination that's impressive, do your best to manage people and reward results.

However, when you begin with the 'Why in Mind,' it moves your focus to the journey that's important, where you manage expectations and reward effort. Only when you begin with the 'why in mind' can you achieve the level beyond success, insuring that you don't just get what you want, but you want what you get, so you don't die with your music still in you.

Bottom line. When the things we believe in and think about are different than the things we do, we will never be happy. And because we can't coach results – we can only coach behavior, and behavior is 100 percent created, driven and sustained by our expectations, both personal motivation and our ability to inspire others comes from our ability to align our internal expectations with our outside actions.

To illustrate and as I wrote about in my book "The Art of Significant Leadership and Talent Development," a thermostat is an instrument that focuses on inside conditions, which measures changes in circumstances that allow us to accurately predict and expect what the temperature will be. A thermostat is a component of a HVAC (heating and air conditioning) control system that senses the difference between actual temperature and the desired *"set-point"* temperature, which then switches the heating or cooling devices on or off, to maintain the previously decided upon correct temperature. The moment you set the thermostat it triggers the equipment to run at full capacity until the *set-point* temperature is reached, shutting off until it's needed again.

In terms of our "human set point," it is always dialed into the level of our self-esteem, sense of self worth and degree of personal development.

For example, how many times have we seen someone win 100 million dollars in the lottery and three years later they are flat broke? How many people do we know who go on a crazy diet and lose fifty pounds or more and six months later they have gained all the weight back and more. Why is this?

It is simply because of their 'personal thermostat' – no matter what happens on the outside with money, weight, relationships, promotions of authority, etc., ultimately our thermostat is going to kick in to bring our outside world to match our internal 'set point.' In order to accumulate more in the outside world, the key to this equation is to 'become' more on the inside.

In order to climb your career and social ladders to reach the highest circle of influence, you must first raise your 'set point' by learning the language of leadership at that level, while matching their levels of education, skill set training, social graces, attire and recreational preferences before they will invite you to join their ranks (as in the 1960-70's television sitcom "Beverly Hillbillies' who never progressed because they continued to dress like 'hicks' and call their swimming pool a 'cement pond.')

What the 'Hillbillies' should have done is taken their extraordinary marksmanship expertise as hunters and joined a prestigious gun club (buying and wearing the faddish gun club attire), and their incredible riding skills and joined a polo club (which would have required that they wear the team uniforms, and learn to appreciate their preferred restaurants, food, drinks and charitable organizations for which they could now volunteer). This would have given them immediate credibility and acceptance into the 'privileged society.' And just as an immigrant who comes to America and enrolls in "ESL' classes to learn to speak English, had the Hillbillies listened more than they talked, over time they could have changed their 'hayseed slang and backwoods ways' into grammatically correct communication, which is one of the most important keys to 'achieving the level beyond success.'

In terms of personal and professional performance, behavior is driven by two kinds of expectations: Internal and External. Internal expectations are set for ourselves by ourselves and usually seek instant gratification. External expectations are set by others and usually seek long-term results.

Our ability to delay gratification is a master skill; a triumph of the reasoning brain over the impulsive brain; a sign of emotional intelligence and stability that comes by being held accountable to high expectations.

Chapter Six

The Art Of Creating Your 'What' And 'How-To'

"Don't just learn from your own mistakes – learn from other people's mistakes. To increase your productivity you shrink your learning curve by shortening the distance between point A and point B."

—Dan Clark

ONCE YOU IDENTIFY your 'personal why' it is critical that you now turn your clearly defined 'why' and compelling 'want' (passionate goal) into a passionate 'what' and step-by-step action plan. Obviously this means that the quickest way to is to turn your successful sales career into a significant sales 'calling,' is to learn a time-tested system and commit to following it, knowing that because it worked for other significant sales professionals, it will also work for you. Champions are not born – they are made; you don't coach results – you coach behavior.

Therefore, not only do you need to figure out the proper steps you must follow to get from where you are to where you want to be, but you must also figure out the pattern of the program and the sequential order in which you take the steps that will guarantee an increase in your personal performance.

The following self-administered game/exercise will prove how by first seeking to understand a system and its specific step-by-step orderly pattern of performance, you really can shorten your learning curve and increase your productivity.

ORDER

When you look around our world you will notice there is a definite 'order' in the universe, generated in our lives by regimens, which are concrete, clear, intelligent, and rigorously pursued performance mechanisms that keep us on track.

Some call these regimens righteous routines; others look at them as iron rods that they can hold on to that will take them from where they are to where they want to be. Personally, I call these routines "patterns"—and I am deliberate about that language.

Routines and rods are man-made systems based on who is right. It's "You do this because I said so," regardless of whether the routine is good, better, great, best, or right.

The patterns I am speaking of already exist in the universe. Based on what is right, which is revealed through our conscience, they give us quick and constant access to the universe's governing powers.

Patterns exist for becoming an exemplary leader or a competent mother; for increasing sales or for creating extraordinary customer experiences; for winning a political election; or for accomplishing an array of other goals. Those who discover the patterns simplify every process, increase productivity, and attain results quicker.

If you first were told why you needed to do something and were then told what needed to be done and when, would this change your desire to obey?

If you were then shown the specific pattern, time-tested, step-by-step plan of action and proven formula to accomplish your assigned task, would this change your desire to obey? Why? How?

PATTERNS

Time yourself for two minutes and see how many numbers you can find in sequential order starting with #1, then find #2, then 3, 4, 5 and so on until you have located all 100 numbers.

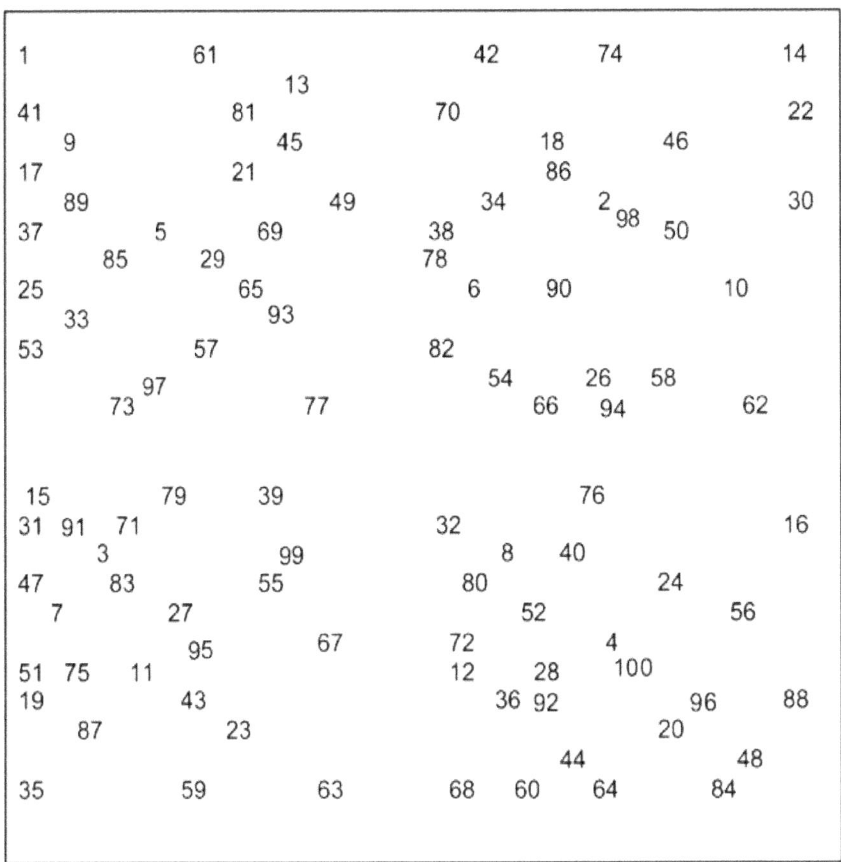

How many numbers did you locate? On the next page is a replica chart that has been divided into four quadrants. Once you figure out the orderly pattern that was used to create the chart, your speed, efficiency, and effectiveness in finding the numbers increases dramatically. Starting in the upper left box locate 1. In the upper right box is 2. In the lower left box is 3. In the lower right box is 4. Back up to the upper left box you'll find 5, and so on. Time yourself again for one minute and compare your score.

```
┌─────────────────────────────────┬─────────────────────────────────┐
│ 1              61               │      42        74           14  │
│                      13         │                                 │
│ 41             81               │ 70                          22  │
│    9              45            │         18        46            │
│ 17            21                │         86                      │
│    89             49            │      34      2       30         │
│ 37      5      69               │ 38            98   50           │
│       85     29                 │ 78                              │
│ 25            65                │    6     90            10       │
│    33             93            │                                 │
│ 53         57                   │ 82                              │
│          97                     │      54      26   58            │
│        73        77             │         66    94        62      │
├─────────────────────────────────┼─────────────────────────────────┤
│ 15         79      39           │               76                │
│ 31 91   71                      │ 32                          16  │
│      3                          │       8      40                 │
│ 47      83         99           │    80               24          │
│    7         27    55           │         52              56      │
│            95         67        │ 72            4                 │
│ 51 75   11                      │ 12      28      100             │
│ 19            43                │    36 92          96        88  │
│    87         23                │                   20           │
│                                 │         44             48       │
│ 35         59         63        │ 68   60      64      84         │
└─────────────────────────────────┴─────────────────────────────────┘
```

Awesome game/exercise, eh? How many more numbers did you find and circle once you knew the 'system?' Will you now commit to learning and meticulously following a time-tested, proven sales system?

Chapter Seven
The Art Of Gardening

"We don't see things as they are. We see things as we are. If two people are looking out the same window at the same rainstorm and one horribly frowns and the other beautifully smiles, the weather did not change."

—Dan Clark

A MAN HAD a dream in which a genie came to him and explained that because he had lived a noble life, he would grant him one wish. The man thought for a minute and said, "I wish for peace and happiness and prosperity to fill the whole earth." The genie smiled and replied, "That's an honorable wish, sir, but we don't deal in fruits here, we only deal in seeds."

As I've traveled the world for the last thirty years and interfaced with millions of people in every industry and socioeconomic condition on the planet, I have noticed that most people only focus on and talk about results and fruits instead of the seeds that caused and produced them.

A classic example of this is showcased every time we injure our bodies. If we twist and snap something in our knee and don't immediately go to a doctor to help us fix what is broken, because we are limping, it throws our back out of alignment and our back starts to hurt. After a while our back is so painful that we finally go to a spine specialist. But because it is our knee that is injured, and he is not aware of this, he can find nothing wrong with our back, and therefore, misdiagnoses our condition and only gives us medication to mask the pain. Hmm.

Doctors call this, "referred pain" where our discomfort is manifested somewhere in our body other than its real source. When it comes to getting and staying physically healthy and well we must always fix what is *really* broken. In other words, we must scratch where it itches. If your elbow itches, you don't scratch your nose to stop the irritation.

If I was to ask you what is broken in your life, what would you tell me? And if I asked you what you were doing to fix it, what would you explain? Have your troubles and challenges been misdiagnosed?

Misdiagnosis is happening everywhere. For example, the school-based cases of ADD and ADHD (Attention Disorder), have risen 66% since 2005. ADD and ADHD are frontal lobe brain disorders, which is the part of the brain that plays a key role in higher mental functions such as motivation and social behavior. Are you telling me that out of nowhere, 66% of our youth have a frontal lobe problem? Where did that come from?

No. This medical prognosis is a gross malpractice misdiagnosis that we should definitely discuss on another day. But FYI – Albert Einstein, Thomas Edison, Charles Lindberg, Henry Ford, John D. Rockefeller, Andrew Carnegie, Steven Jobs, Bill Gates, and Sir Richard Branson all share the misdiagnosis of ADD/ADHD.

In my home state of Utah our doctors prescribe 400% more Prozac for depression than doctors prescribe in any other state in the U.S. Are you kidding me? Utah has spectacular mountains to climb, rivers to fish, trails to hike, national parks to visit, and amazing and friendly, family focused residents who seek education and give service before self. There is no way that we have 400% more depressed people in Utah than in any other state! This is blatant and irresponsible misdiagnosis!!

The good news is that if your body breaks, when you go to the right doctor and he gives you the correct diagnoses, and he performs the necessary surgery or non-surgical procedures to stimulate your body to start healing itself, when you go through the proper steps of rehabilitation, the broken part of your body becomes stronger and more stable than it was before you injured it.

The same thing holds true for our attitudes, behaviors, broken hearts, shattered dreams, and how our life is turning out. If you think your life is in shambles and nothing like you want it to be, all you need to do is itemize what specific thing or things are broken, and find the right attitude doctor and behavioral specialist who can give you the correct diagnoses and rehabilitation plan, and help you help yourself fix it.

Do you know anyone who is not scratching where it itches? Do you know anyone who is getting sour fruits and negative results they don't want, and at the same time seeking sweet fruits and positive results that they will never get because they have not planted the specific seeds that will produce them?

Happiness – Found or Created?

As I travel the world I ask everybody I meet what they are looking for in life. Everybody always answers, "Happiness and Success." Sounds good, but it creates two major challenges:

#1: Happiness is a fruit, not a seed. Happiness isn't something you discover, it's something you create. Happiness is not a destination of success, arriving somewhere impressive. It's a journey of creating significant relevance so you are valued now and important forever.

When you are not valued, you are not happy. When you are not happy, you don't feel significant. When you don't feel significant, you die before you're dead.

It is my experience that because we have allowed Hollywood to define 'happiness' as a shallow focus on celebrity, power and fortune, society in general relentlessly pursues 'counterfeit happiness,' which is nothing more than the momentary highs that come from an alcohol buzz, hit of illegal drugs, prescription medication abuse, casual sexual encounters, adrenalin adventures, a raise and promotion at work, and the fleeting ego arrogance that accompanies fame, authority and money.

Because our multimillion-dollar free enterprise marketing and propaganda machine has convinced most of us that material advantages readily translate into social and emotional benefits, most allow their psychic energy to become invested in material goals that distort and destroy their sensitivity toward the most meaningful rewards such as friendship, art, literature, natural beauty, spirituality, and the reality that family structure bound together in a two parent home filled with unconditional love is what creates real, authentic, and lasting happiness.

#2: Success is also a fruit, not a seed, and is defined as "producing results." This is good news to the masses because it means everybody is successful because everybody produces results. However, because failure and losing are also results, being successful is not enough. Our sights must always be set on achieving desired results.

Bottom line. Successful people get what they want. But those of us who are seeking to live a life of significance are doing everything we know how to do to make sure we want what we get, so we don't die before we are dead.

To illustrate: During one particularly long, harsh winter, the snowfall in Utah was so deep that it forced the deer population out of the mountains and into the parks and residential areas in search of food. Because the deer were stranded, state wildlife agencies immediately brought in truckloads of hay and spread it in the fields around our neighborhood so the deer could eat. One week later more than a hundred dead deer were lying in the streets. Why?

When the veterinarians performed autopsies, they discovered that the stomachs of the deer were full of hay. The deer had eaten plenty of food, but they had not been nourished. They got what they thought they wanted at the moment, but they died because they didn't get what they truly needed.

By planting positive seeds in our cause-and-effect world in which we live that will continually grow into magnificent trees that will outlive us and constantly bring forth positive fruit and desired significant results every day, you will leave a long-lasting legacy that connects us all together in the family of humanity.

This is what it means to transform from successful to significant, and into living Life Unlimited where you attract and maintain wonderful relationships, good health, have more than enough money to share, and are genuinely happy because you have enough time to pursue your passion and the resources to leave your family, friends, community and world in better shape than you found them!

Bottom line. American founding father Thomas Jefferson best illuminates the significance of mastering the Art of Gardening as his interest in flowers and planting can be dated to 1766, when he began documenting his naturalistic observations in his *Garden Book*. As a connoisseur of trees, flowers and gardening techniques the "Gardens of Monticello" were designed and planted by Jefferson on his plantation near Charlottesville, Virginia and included a flower garden, a fruit orchard, and a vegetable garden, which showcased many exotic seeds and plants from his travels abroad.

And when it comes to our individual responsibility to the Art of Gardening, Jefferson said, "I'm not really a career person. I'm a gardener, basically, who knows we can complain because rose bushes have thorns, or rejoice because thorn bushes have roses. Though an old man, I am but a young gardener. A society grows great when old men plant trees whose shade they know they shall never sit in. Too old to plant trees for my own gratification, I shall do it for my posterity."

Eric Hoffer profoundly adds, "The individual's most vital need is to prove his worth, and this usually means an insatiable hunger for action wherein he develops and employs his capacities and talents through love, admiration, and genuine interest in the life of another."

Significant Individuals Automatically Connect and Compliment

To illustrate: A young man literally changes the world with a significant invention, but he admits that he was led to a life of inventing by a certain book he had read. So, to whom do we owe our debt of gratitude for enriching our lives so significantly with this invention? The inventor? Or the author of the book who the inventor freely admits led him to a life of inventing in the first place?

Or should we thank the teacher who encouraged the child to become an author? Certainly without the teacher the book never would have been written.

Or is the world indebted to the extremely successful businesswoman who sought to live a life of abundance by creating the scholarship fund that allowed a poor, underserved girl to attend college and become the teacher who encouraged her student to become the author of the book that inspired the man whose invention changed the world?

Or should we thank the doctor who saved the life of a mother, who several years later bore the child who became the businesswoman living a life of abundance, who created the college scholarship?

Or maybe the one who really deserves our deepest appreciation is the hardworking delivery man who because he was living an abundant life, drove the wagon that carried the lumber that was used to build the doctor's office, where the doctor saved the woman who, several years later, bore the child who grew up to create the scholarship fund that allowed the disadvantaged student to attend college and become a teacher who inspired her young student to study writing and write a book that inspired the inventor to change the world.

CHAPTER EIGHT

THE ART OF TRANSFORMING 'CHANGE' INTO 'STRETCHING'

"All knowledge is recollection. When I say something profound and people nod their heads in agreement, I'm not teaching them anything new. They are recalling something they already learned in a previous experience. The answers have always been and still are in the box!"

—Dan Clark

"Don't wish it was easier; wish you were better. If you are not willing to risk the unusual, you will have to settle for the ordinary. The few who do are the envy of the many who only watch."

—Jim Rohn

DO YOU SEE that 'change' from the outside in is reactive and creates 'pressure?' Do you agree that 'change' from the outside in creates a 'victim mentality' where it's, 'whoa me, life isn't fair,' whine, complain, blame and moan, that continuously proves that 'miserable being finds other miserable being, then they are happy?' If so, do you also see that 'change' from the inside out is proactive and creates power? Which means it is self-motivated where we feel compelled to change, not because it is expected by others, but because it is demanded of ourselves. Which means it is not change at all – but rather 'stretching' to reach our full potential and become everything we were born to be!

Think about this. No matter what – you will make a lousy somebody else! You are so unique that no one else in the world has your same fingerprints and DNA. Which means, you don't have to change. You need to simply become more of who you already are!

When someone tells you to change, they are suggesting that you were born flawed, and if you attend a seminar or counsel with a psychologist you can put in what was left out at birth. No! This is incorrect. You don't have to change. And no you don't have to exceed your potential. No one can exceed his potential. We just misjudge it! The goal and the purpose of life is to become more of who we already are by becoming better today than we were yesterday until we reach our full capacity and potential as a human being!

CAN'T COACH RESULTS – CAN ONLY COACH BEHAVIOR

The difference is in the fact that you can't coach results—you can only coach behavior. You can't tell your children to get good grades in school, your employees to sell more, your players to win the game, or your troops to defeat the enemy. You can only coach them to set high expectations and to put in the necessary practice time to improve their attitudes and confidence, and perfect their skills and behavior so that winning takes care of itself.

In business, we can't offer a raise every time we want someone to take productivity to the next level.

We can't motivate military or political leaders to increase their performance with money or recognition either. We can motivate them to continue down the road toward significance only by expressing expectations—and not just any expectations but expectations pegged to their own noble quest, their dream, their purpose.

What are your current expectations in the physical, mental, spiritual, emotional, social, financial, and familial sides of your life? How high is your bar compared to your potential? Who is stretching you?

Because all the strengthening occurs in the area past the point of discomfort, and none of us can stretch ourselves to our ultimate capacity as human beings all by ourselves, we all need someone to raise our bar and, most important, to ask us to jump!

We also must dedicate ourselves to going above and beyond the right now—even if we're afraid or otherwise resistant. Obviously we can't jump higher than we are currently able, but still we must keep jumping.

If you want to get better at doing push-ups, you get better and stronger by doing push-ups. It's easier to act our way into positive thinking than to think our way into positive action. Self-esteem, desire, and motivation are not required to change behavior. We need to change what we're doing—behavior changes behavior! When do most people fix their health problems? When it's too late. When do most people read a book on relationships? When their relationships are falling apart.

We don't need to feel motivated to do motivated! It is not enough for us to be empathetic; we must do empathetic. It's not enough for our company to be customer-centric; we must do extraordinary customer service. We can't just be trustworthy, loyal, helpful, friendly, courteous, kind, obedient, cheerful, thrifty, brave, clean, reverent, unconditionally loving, and forgiving; we must do them!

It's not enough for us to be a successful sales professional—we must do significance!

Stretching

Although deciding to stretch is a personal decision, we can stretch ourselves only so far on our own. Stretching requires that someone not merely take us past the point of discomfort but also support us as we hold ourselves in a zone of discomfort so that we can strengthen ourselves to the point that we don't flip back to where we were physically, mentally, spiritually, and emotionally before we started to stretch.

This process is best understood and implemented using the Vertical Stretching Scale that applies to every aspect of our lives:

10

2

3

4

5

6

7

8

9

1

Vertical Stretching Scale

Obviously, the first step is to start where we are. Next, we push and strain ourselves to the point of discomfort. Third, we ask someone we trust and respect to stretch us past the point of discomfort and support us there until the strain and stretch are no longer stressful.

Once we have grown comfortable at the 7, 8, and 9 levels, they become our new starting points, the new normal, and on our revised, amped-up scale, we start again at 1.

Now the level that used to be 10 becomes level 6—no longer the snapping point but instead the targeted point of discomfort, which we now can handle and surpass with support. Too many of us want to stretch and strengthen all at once. Leaders set outrageously high, unrealistic goals without giving even a modest amount of support. Then they blame their people when they snap and fall.

I know a lot of superstar athletes, corporate executives, military leaders, and professionals in every field who will verify that all strengthening occurs in the area past the point of discomfort. While you can get to the point of discomfort on your own, you need someone else whom you admire and respect to push you past that point and then support you there while you become stronger.

If you're a Sales Manager, now is the time to ask yourself just what you are demanding of your people. Do they realistically have what they need from you to grow? Or are you just setting them up to snap right back to where they were the minute you, as their "physical therapist," stop pushing and pulling?

Being Stretched and Stretching Others Through Influence

This metaphor of physical therapy is at the heart and soul of what it means to be a sales leader. At the end of the day, what qualifies someone to be a called a leader is not a title. It's that person's capacity to influence others to stretch their minds (attitudes) and behaviors in order to achieve important, significant results.

Most believe the word influence is synonymous with the less impressive and more suspicious tool called persuasion. It's not. Persuasive stretching is not about allowing someone to apply the right combination of verbal tricks to get us to change, or to equip us as fast-talking manipulators who use stealthy tactics to exert our will over others.

Stretching is about making winning personal and influencing yourself and others to take the required and necessary steps to get from where you are to where you want to be, regardless of the effort or how long it takes.

The good news is that in order to create profound and lasting change, you don't have to stretch fifty behaviors. You usually have to stretch only one or two key behaviors and leverage them. This means stretching is more than focusing on vague results, such as "We need to empower our employees," "Create a culture of excellence," "Help troubled teenagers," "Build a team," and "Improve customer service."

Improving customer service could be interpreted as anything from answering the phone by the second ring to giving each customer a $200 jacket. Stretching is having a clear determination of what specific behaviors to change and having a clear understanding of what strategies to implement in order to actually change those behaviors.

FROM CHANGE MODE TO STRETCH MODE

The discouraging challenge of change is that those who focus only on changing usually talk about the results they want, but until they decide exactly how they're going to measure those results, they remain nothing more than ideas. Changing is simple when you're trying to gain or lose weight, which you measure by getting on a scale; or when you're trying to measure profitability, which you determine by calculating income minus expenses.

However, in order to improve and track more significant things like integrity, morale, loyalty, respect, duty, honor, personal courage, customer satisfaction, employee engagement, and a culture of excellence, such items must be quantified into something that represents the idea or value that can be measured.

Using the Vertical Stretching Scale, and in concert with the highest universal laws of Obedience, Perseverance, and Seeking The Whole Truth, stretching first requires identifying a passionate why, which illuminates the want, what, how, and when, with specific feedback measurement and strict accountability.

Measurement won't drive behavior if it doesn't maintain your undivided attention, and it definitely won't maintain your attention if it's rarely assessed. This means that stretching is the highest form of continuous improvement and the only rapid growth strategy that actually works to create both short- and long-term desired results.

Chapter Nine

The Art Of Paying The Price
"The Answers Are Still In The Box"

"No Pain, No Gain really means No Heart, No Chance. Which means when you are prepared you shall not fear; which means F.E.A.R. doesn't mean: 'Forget Everything And Run.' FEAR means: 'Face Everything And Rise' knowing that courage is being scared to death, and saddling up anyway."

—Dan Clark

Everybody wants to win and become a Significant Sales and Marketing Professional, but very few are willing to Prepare to become such. Very few are willing to pay the price today (and every day) so they can enjoy the 'prize' forever. Why?

They think it's going to require a massive change over a long drawn out process, so they talk themselves out of it, rationalizing again and again that they really don't need this change and therefore, decide the 'juice is not worth the squeeze,' and out of fear and lack of conviction never commence to begin to start!

How sad and deplorably unacceptable! Especially when the difference between good and great is just a little bit of extra effort – the difference between an average Sales Professional and a Significant Sales and Marketing Champion is only a small amount of additional effort. For example, in baseball, what does it mean to have a .200 batting average? You hit safely on base two out of ten times up to bat. Because this is relatively easy these players make minimum salary, never do television commercials with endorsement deals, and are traded from team to team as often as a manager changes his dirty socks! In contrast, what does it mean to have a .300 batting average? Obviously you hit safely on base three out of every ten times up to bat. But because this is more difficult you make maximum salary, get your share of endorsement deals, and you become the labeled 'franchise player' who gets all of the organization's marketing benefits and community perks.

This means the difference between a .200 hitter and a .300 hitter – an unsuccessful minimum requirement mediocre guy and a very successful, maximum effort super star is only one hit in every ten times up to bat. And if they let each at bat go to full count, with three balls and two strikes, the difference between a .200 hitter and a .300 hitter is only one hit in every sixty pitches! The difference between good and great – between success and significance is just a little bit of extra effort. So... what's holding you back?

Yes, the toughest step is always the first, and oftentimes the decision to 'go' takes the longest, but in order to get a hit you must first swing the bat. And in order to become a super star hitter you must learn what pitches are better to hit than others, so you can take advantage of the opportunities thrown your way, swing with confidence and get more hits. That's it. Simple.

For example, a famous shoe manufacturer in England sent two sales representatives to Africa to see if there might be an opportunity to open up a new market and sell more shoes. Both reps returned to London and reported. The first sales professional said, 'Nobody in Africa wears shoes. So, there is no market for our products there.' The second sales professional said, 'Nobody in Africa wears shoes. So, there's a *huge* market for our products in Africa!'

The fundamental truth is: when your attitude is right, your ability will always catch up. For example, at the elementary level in the mystical world of numerology, each letter is assigned a number. The letter A is 1, B is 2, C is 3, and so on until Z is 26. Just for fun, I wrote out the words KNOWLEDGE, HARDWORK, and ATTITUDE, matching up the letters with their corresponding numbers. What I discovered is a self-standing, self-supporting motivational message:

KNOWLEDGE
$11 + 14 + 15 + 23 + 12 + 5 + 4 + 7 + 5 = 96\%$

HARDWORK
$8 + 1 + 18 + 4 + 23 + 15 + 18 + 11 = 98\%$

ATTITUDE
$1 + 20 + 20 + 9 + 20 + 21 + 4 + 5 = 100\%$

Attitude means 100%, giving it everything you've got when less would be sufficient. It's playing the football game for all 60 minutes. It's leaning over your plate for all twelve bites of your spaghetti dinner so you don't spill tomato sauce down the front of your white sweater on the last bite. Attitude is about self-discipline. Discipline means obeying others; self discipline means obeying yourself 100% of the time with a firm commitment to do whatever it takes. Having a Positive Mental Attitude (PMA) is knowing that it's not what happens to you, it's what you do with what happens to you that makes you a champion!

Remember: Attitude really is everything. When your attitude is right, your abilities will always catch up. You can, only when you think you can. Because every situation has a positive and a negative way to look at it, it is critical to always take the high road and choose to be positive. If you think you can or can't you are absolutely right!

EVERYTHING YOU NEED
IS ALREADY INSIDE OF YOU

Greek philosopher Plato taught, "All knowledge is recollection." Which means that whenever I address an audience and say something profound, and people nod their heads in agreement, I am not teaching them anything new. They are simply recalling something they already learned in a previous experience.

For this reason, the next time you hear someone suggest "You've got to think outside the lines—you've got to think outside the box," join me in challenging the status quo and ask, "What if the answers are still IN the box?"

Most people who enroll in training courses come in search of the new answers, when we should be coming in search of the right answers—not always found by seeking answers to questions, but by questioning answers, which then reveal that the right answers have always been right or we can't call them right.

This means everything you need to take yourself to the next level is already inside of you. Everything required to take your organization to the next level is already inside of it. You should look for what is, and not for what you think should be.

You do not become more organized by purchasing a filing cabinet. You do not become more healthy by joining a gym. You don't become more at ease in your life by speaking with a therapist.

You shouldn't say, "If I could only find a new job, then I would be successful; if I could just lose this extra weight, then everything would be okay; if I could just make this relationship work, then I would be happy; if I could just buy me new golf clubs, then my game would improve."

In the gun control controversy it is clear that when you put a loaded gun on a table, it could lay there for years until someone picks it up and pulls the trigger. Guns don't kill people—people kill people. You don't blame Boeing for the planes hitting the World Trade Center Towers on September 11—you don't blame spoons for people getting fat!

Obviously, because we all have been conditioned from an early age to look outward—to look to others for approval, acceptance, self-worth, expecting something or someone else to solve our problems, we've forgotten to look inside ourselves.

Scratch Where It Itches!

To illustrate: imagine there is a power failure in your home—the lights go out, you can't see a thing, and you drop your keys. You look around for a moment but can't find them in the dark.

However, you notice that the streetlights are on outside, and strangely rationalize that you shouldn't stay inside searching in the dark when there is a light on outside where you can see.

While you're on your hands and knees your neighbor stops and asks what you're doing. You tell him you dropped your keys, so he obviously starts helping you look for them. When he asks where you dropped them and you tell him "in the house," he angrily asks, "Why are you looking outside to solve a problem that's inside?"

When you have a difficulty, struggle and challenge that is located inside of you, do you look for the solution somewhere outside of yourself?

Yes, Einstein said, "No problem can be solved by the same kind of thinking that created it." But thinking that you need something outside of you to get better in order for you to make your life work at a significant level; or thinking that you need to compete against something or someone else until you perform better than them in order to feel successful, is the same kind of delusional thinking that created your pain, struggle, confusion and lack of success in the first place.

Different thinking isn't "thinking outside the box." It is realizing that when you change the way you look at things, the things you look at change. It's embracing Native American wisdom realizing: "the answers are in the forest, in the sweat lodge, in the soul—discovering how strong you are only when being strong is the only choice you have." It's understanding something we all know but seldom remind ourselves about: "Scratch Where It Itches." If your nose itches you don't scratch your elbow. Duh! The practical application of these truths is showcased by competing fast-food restaurants who occupy all four corners of the same intersection. They want to feed off of each other's traffic, and use their competitor's success as a report card for how they are doing in the market, yet they are competing only against themselves.

If one of them goes out of business, it is never the other's fault. It is because of poor leadership, ineffective management, bad food, horrible customer service, filthy washrooms, and an unreasonable value proposition.

When we are not the very best we can possibly be so as to differentiate ourselves from our friends, teammates and co-workers in good, clean, pure, powerful, positive ways, we are forced to compete at the lowest common denominators of price and politics, which are based on who is right instead of what is right.

When you believe the answers are outside of yourself, you begin your desired progress with the "how" in mind, which quickly defaults to focusing on the "end in mind," which denies you the power that comes from identifying your personal "why."

Remember: When the things you believe in and think deeply about are different than the things you do, you will never be happy or achieve significance—"A house divided against itself cannot stand."—"Look not on his countenance, or on the height of his stature; because I have refused him: for the Lord sees not as man sees; for man looks on the outward appearance, but the Lord looks on the heart."—"Then I heard the voice of the Lord saying, "Whom shall I send? And who will go for us?" And I said, "Here am I. Send me!" (Mark 3:25; I Samuel 16:7; Isaiah 6:8).

Because the goal is not to change, but to become more of who you already are, the answers to conquering your fears, defeating your limiting beliefs, intensifying your personal growth, and magnifying your leadership opportunities are inside of you!

I submit to you that everything required to take yourself to the next level is already inside of you. All you need to do is associate with the right people who will challenge your limiting beliefs, refuse to accept your self-defeating excuses, question your fear of failure, and remind you about the difference between a scarcity mentality (there is only enough success for me) and an abundance mentality (there is more than enough significance for me and everybody else in the world).

Bottom line. The answers and processes to help us change and reach our potential are not found outside of us. We don't need another assignment and/or another twelve steps to, or seven habits of to help us achieve our goals. Everything required to take ourselves to the next level is already inside of us – especially when we feel we are stressed.

Welcoming And Regulating Stress

Have you ever noticed how some people, even "the best" players, who practice and practice and become brilliant at the basics still choke come game time?

Do you know anyone who has stretched from the inside out and has truly become more of who they already are, and yet when it comes time to perform and show what they can do, they fold under pressure taking a school test, undergoing a corporate exam, or playing in a big game? Why do you think this happens?

Have you noticed how stress even affects some "right" leaders, coaches, employees, and players but seemingly not others? Why do you think this occurs?

When the external circumstance is the same for everybody competing and involved, it is clear that talent and experience don't explain differences in performance. The one and only thing we can control is stress.

As already mentioned, pressure is not something that is naturally there. It's created when you question your own ability. When you know what you can do, there is no question. Even when you know you are over your head, pressure is not stress.

The internal impact that stress has on an individual physically and mentally varies greatly among individuals and plays a huge role in performance level. In competition, stress is the only thing that can be controlled to a high degree.

Research produced the well-known *Yerkes-Dodson Law*, diagramed below:

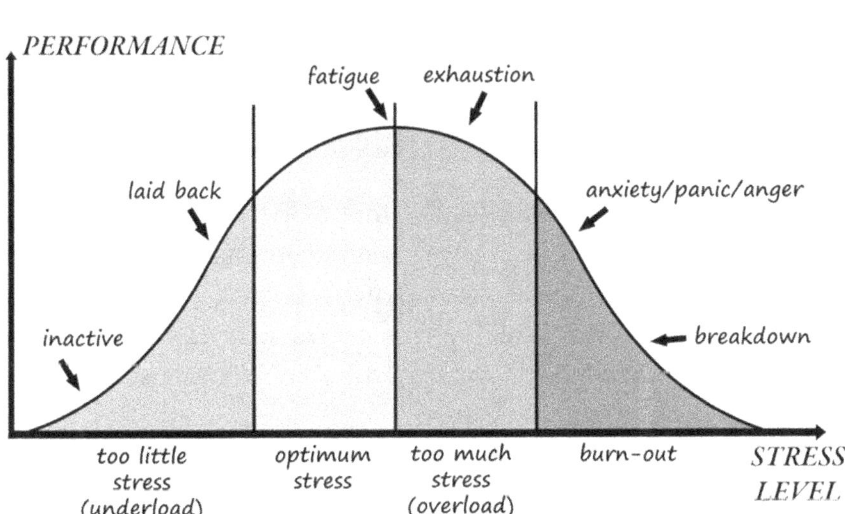

From this diagram it is obvious, and extremely important to remember, that stress and performance are always linked. Stress facilitates performance. Too little stress causes weak performance. However, too much stress is debilitating. Peak performance comes as we seek balance. We must seek the optimal level of stress.

Surely we are all different in how much stress we can handle. The goal is to push ourselves to our highest degree of intensity so that we may perform at our ultimate capacity and reach our full potential.

But how will we know when we have gone past the level of optimal stress? It's about the simple law of diminishing returns. We can water a tomato plant only so much. At full capacity, when the plant needs no more water, additional watering only diminishes its growth. Once the water level reaches an optimal level, the effectiveness of water quickly diminishes and eventually kills the tomato plant, head aches, chest pain, decreased libido, high blood pressure, high cholesterol, and an increase in drug and alcohol use.

Performance-related signs are even more obvious and noticeable, including decreased concentration, resulting in increased errors. Because these conditions drain our energy, stress simultaneously tells other costly physical processes – including digestion, reproduction, physical growth, and some aspects of the immune system – to shut down or slow down, making us more susceptible to illnesses ranging from the common cold to cancer. Chronic stress has been linked to heart disease, strokes, depression, Type 2 diabetes, and Post Traumatic Stress.

WHEN STRESS IS BAD

If you're worried about your health, stop. Worry only makes it worse. Warning signs of pushing ourselves past the optimal level of stress include heartburn, appetite changes, irritable bowel, itchy skin, nervous habits such as nail biting, talking way too fast and way too much, insomnia, causes us to tense up, tear up, or go quiet because of the fear of having to live through it again.

When Stress Is Good

There are three ways to maximize performance:

1. Physical management of stress.

2. Cognitive management of stress.

3. Behavioral management of stress.

Physical Management

Diet

Increase your intake of B-complex and C vitamins, which stress depletes. Vitamin deficiency makes the nervous system more reactive, decreasing your ability to control stress. Eat more cereals, leafy green vegetables, liver, fish, citrus fruits, tomatoes, cabbage, and potatoes. Drink more water. Drink less alcohol, which tends to disturb sleep and dehydrate your body. During pressure-packed, stressful situations, it is also critical to decrease caffeine and nicotine intake. As stimulants, they tend to produce an enhanced stress-like response.

Exercise

Increase regularity of exercise during high stress. Exercise burns unhealthy physical byproducts of stress, including increased blood sugar. Exercise improves sleep, provided you exercise three or more hours before attempting to sleep.

Rest

It is essential to everybody's physical, mental, and emotional health to take breaks during the day. Get away from your desk; don't eat lunch there. We need a minimum of two ten-minute breaks per day. Relaxation is productive. We need a minimum of thirty minutes per day, especially at the end of the day. Weekends are meant to recharge us from our stressful week.

Cognitive Management

We must reframe stressors as challenges by changing our descriptive words from problem (which sounds insurmountable) to challenge (which says, "Bring it on!").

This simple alteration in thinking signals the possibility of mastery or gain and establishes a focus on the value of effort. The positive outcome of this reappraisal is the resolution that stressful encounters can be and should be favorable and successful. The result is a new pride, new skill or resource, and new personal growth.

Behavioral Management

You must make an active effort to solve or manage your challenges. This is different from worrying. Remember, "It's easier to act your way into positive thinking than to think your way into positive action." In other words: I'll feel like it when I do it! The fastest way to reduce and eliminate stress is to stop procrastinating, plan, gather information, make decisions, acquire resources, and most significantly, create and write out your personal and organizational 'Credo' you commit to live by.

Chapter Ten

The Art Of Customizing Your Education

"Life responds to deserve and not to need. It doesn't say, 'If you need, you will reap.' It says, 'If you plant, you will reap.' Successful people believe formal education will make them a living. Significant individuals know self-education will make us a fortune. Poor people have big TVs – rich people have big libraries!"

—Jim Rohn (R.I.P. my friend and mentor)

SELF-EDUCATION IS THE new MBA. Knowledge is power, but knowledge has no heart. We don't learn to know – we learn to do. It doesn't do us any good to know how to read if we never pull out a book and read it. All the information in the world isn't going to make a person successful. It's like the guy who has three PhDs: one in philosophy, one in psychology, one in sociology. He doesn't have a job but at least he can explain why! Reason leads to conclusions, but it is emotion that leads to action. A lot of people know smoking is bad for our health, but they smoke anyway. Many know that a career in Sales and Marketing will give and get them an abundant life unlimited they know they deserve, but they refuse to hang in there and work the system long enough to turn their knowledge into reality.

Therefore, to motivate your self to take the chance because the reward outweighs the risk, I make this suggestion:

Instead of wasting precious time listening to the radio or watching TV, we can redirect that time to a very good use. We can listen to CDs and tune into the internet almost anytime: while driving in our car, exercising, jogging, taking walks, shaving, getting dressed in the morning, flying cross country or riding the subway; it's an extremely easy way to acquire knowledge of just about any subject.

For example, during the last few years I have enjoyed listening to experts teach me about: Spirituality, Philosophy, Apologetics, Marriage counseling, Improving communication skills, Public speaking, How to deal with difficult people, Closing sales and marketing, Leadership skills, Time management, How to win friends, influence people and negotiate to a win/win, Public relations, Foreign languages, Health and nutrition, Vocabulary building, and more!

There are literally hundreds of subjects that can be learned by merely listening to recorded speeches. For me, the best place to listen and learn is in my car. According to the American Automobile Association, the average American car owner drives between 12,000 and 25,000 miles a year. This translates into 500 to 1,000 hours each year that we spend in our car, or the equivalent of 12 to 25 forty-hour work-weeks.

My friend and colleague Brian Tracy, an international speaker on time management, suggests that in order to make maximum use of our time, we turn our car into a "university on wheels", and never have it moving without an instructional motivational message playing.

Imagine, having 500 to 1,000 hours every year for continued adult education. That's the equivalent of spending three to six months a year in classes, or taking one to two full university semesters each year.

A few years ago, UCLA conducted a study, which found that if you commute to work in a metropolitan area and listen to programs in your car, you can gain the equivalent of three years of college education in four years time. Audio learning has been called the greatest breakthrough in education since the invention of the printing press. Listening to a 90-minute recorded speech is equivalent to reading 40 pages of a book, which means when you do it every day, it is the equivalent of reading a 250-page book every week, which equates to reading

52 books a year or 520 books in 10 years! Listening to two programs every day is the equivalent of reading 1,000 books in 10 years!

In a world where the average person reads only one book a year, (or 10 books in 10 years), if you are really serious about creating yourself into the person you have the potential to be, which will make you stand out in any crowd and give you the competitive advantage in every marketplace, customize your education beginning today and every next 'today!

CHAPTER ELEVEN

THE ART OF THE LAW OF ATTRACTION

"We can't create something out of nothing. Planet earth was brought forth from matter unorganized and assembled according to interactive universal laws that govern its existence. The rules of the emotional, spiritual, and relational universe are equally as demanding as those of the physical universe. Every part of the universe responds only to law. Man did not get to the moon with random trajectories and with each astronaut doing his own thing. The price for reaching the moon was obedience to universal law.

In 1961, when U.S. President John F. Kennedy asked the nation to commit to landing a man on the moon before the end of the decade, few of the most critical specifics were clear. By changing how we think and by understanding the dynamics that actually govern and produce highest-level living, not only do we learn the lesser principles and laws of success that most improvement programs cover, but we also tap into our potential to achieve our greatest results. The potential that is in you and me and working through us right now in the dimension beyond success is what we call significance."

—Dan Clark

WE ATTRACT WHAT WE BELIEVE WE DESERVE

"Wealth flows through you, not to you. You can get anything in this life that you want if you are willing to help enough other people get what they want."

—Dan Clark

ARE YOU ONE of the millions who hate their jobs, only look forward to Friday instead of Monday, and think you are paid by the hour, when in reality we are all paid for the value we bring to that hour? Yes, you have a job that allows you to buy impressive things you think you want at the moment, but someone else is raising your children, you are married to your work, and every day you reluctantly acknowledge that money can't buy happiness, love or self-actualization.

Remember: We become the average of the five people we associate with the most. If you hang out with five broke people, or five negative, cancerous, pessimistic, complaining, blaming whiners, you will be a broke, negative, cancerous, pessimistic, complaining, blaming whiner.

To reiterate, when you put a hard to catch horse in the same field with an easy to catch horse, you usually end up with two hard to catch horses. When you put a sick child in the same room with a healthy child, you usually end up with two sick children. To be disciplined, healthy and significant you need to associate with the disciplined, healthy, and significant. To have the courage to let go of your comfortable past and guaranteed present, and take your shot on doing what you really love right now and in the future, you need to associate with individuals who believe in you until you believe in yourself!

Which means, when you are the smartest, wealthiest, most-clever and most charitable person in your group, you need a new group, based on who you can count 'on,' and who you count 'out!' Because of both the long-term ramifications and short-term rewards and consequences of the Law of Attraction, we must be willing to pay any price and travel any distance to associate with extraordinary human beings.

The Law of Attraction is real and always in play regardless if you want to consciously engage it or not. It's true: 'Birds of a feather flock together.' The Massachusetts Institute of Technology (MIT) did a study, which indicated that we earn within $2000 to $3000 dollars of our closest friends. People rub off on you.

According to a study published in the New England Journal of Medicine, which involved a detailed analysis of a large social network of 12,067 people who had been closely followed for 32 years, from 1971 until 2003, obesity can spread from person to person, much like a virus. When one person gains weight, close friends tend to gain weight too. In this study the investigators knew who was friends with whom, as well as who was a spouse or sibling or neighbor, and they knew how much each person weighed at various times over three decades.

That let them watch what happened over the years as people became obese. Did their friends also become obese? Did family members? Or neighbors?

The answer, the researchers report, was that people were most likely to become obese when a friend became obese. That increased one's chances of becoming obese by 57 percent. It didn't even matter if the friend was hundreds of miles away – the influence remained. And the greatest influence of all was between mutual close friends. If one became obese, the other had a 171 percent increased chance of becoming obese too.

The same effect seemed to occur for weight loss, the investigators say, but since most people were gaining, not losing, over the 32 years, the result was an obesity epidemic. Dr. Nicholas Christakis, a physician and professor of medical sociology at Harvard Medical School and a principal investigator in the new study, says one explanation is that friends affect each other's perception of fatness. When a close friend becomes obese, obesity may not look so bad.

"You change your idea of what is an acceptable body type by looking at the people around you," Christakis said. The investigators say their findings can help explain why Americans became fatter in recent years: Persons who became obese were likely to drag some friends with them. When it comes to the Law of Attraction, if you don't like what you're attracting, simply change what's attracting it. To change what you're attracting, change what you believe you deserve.

The fundamental governing principle of the Law of Attraction is: Likes Attract Likes. You are a magnet, attracting everything to you, and this unfathomable magnetic power is emitted through your thoughts.

A very well-known and well-documented example of the Law of Attraction is the placebo effect, most of which occur in medication trials. Patients who believed they would be affected positively by the medications fared better than those who did not, even when given an inert tablet (often a sugar pill).

Every one of us puts out a measurable energy that falls into a specific frequency that can only be felt by someone on that same frequency. Are you putting out positive or negative energy? Look around. Are you attractive or unattractive? If you don't like your current program and the vibe you're obviously dialed in to, finely-tune who you are, tune in to your true frequency, and start sending that energy out! One wavelength, one frequency, one signal and one vibe can only attract the same wavelength, and same frequency, signal and vibe. "Likes Attract Likes" is a principle of the universe that never changes for anyone or anything.

The next time you're driving down the winding road of life tuned into your program of choice, and for some reason you lose your connection, instead of continuing on and frantically changing your channel to settle for a sub par shallow, temporary program fix that is easily found and commonly heard, why not stop, eliminate the distractions that are blocking your reception, and go where you can hear and feel, fully experience and easily tune back in to the frequency and deeper, meaningful program that you enjoyed before. It is there. The program is always broadcasting. But it is our responsibility to find it and tune into it!

When it comes to the Law of Attraction we must never think it's a 'build it and they will come' proposition. Obeying the Law of Attraction means we are always bettering ourselves to be more interesting and appealing, and actively searching for the individuals who share this same passion, purpose and desire to connect with us. When our energy guides us to each other, and our frequencies perfectly match up, and our communication vibes are strong, and the signals we are transmitting and receiving from each other are coming in loud and clear, it is beautiful at home, at work, at play, on a team, in a business deal, in a military squadron or platoon, in community service, and especially in the arms of our "one and only!" Regardless if it's a personal or professional relationship, our feelings are a feedback mechanism to us about whether we are on track or not, whether we're on course or off course.

Of all the questions you may have, the most important to be clear about are, "What do I want? What is possible to achieve? Do I actually believe I can get it – with my weaknesses and limitations and my strengths? And, do I believe I deserve it?" Honestly answering these inquiries is fundamental in creating and projecting our chosen energy force, wavelength frequency, and continual energy flow. To illustrate, let's talk about the process of purchasing an automobile.

What Do You Deserve In A Car?

The first question is: do you deserve to drive a new car or a used car? Whatever your choice, you immediately notice others driving similar conditioned cars. In my case, a few years ago I decided I deserved to buy me my dream sports car. I was in Hawaii and paid good money to rent a red Ferrari. What a joke! I removed the coupe hard top to make it a convertible, and the windshield came up to my chin. My head stuck out the top and I looked like Mr. Potato Head! I had to duck to drive and couldn't even get it out of first gear!

After much searching I finally discovered the Porsche had plenty of headroom and I decided that I deserved to own and drive one. And what happened when I got "clear" on what kind of a new car I was going to buy? I suddenly started noticing how many cars were like mine on the streets and highways. A guy at the end of my street drives a Porsche and until I knew what I wanted, I had not noticed his car before. Then I got clear on the style I wanted and focused my energies on buying a 911 GT3, fuel injected and turbo-charged with a whale-fin on the back. And do you know what happened? I was blown away by how many 911 GT3 Porsches with a whale-fin on the back there were in my community. Then I got even clearer and decided it should be charcoal grey.

And what happened? Although there weren't a lot of them on the road, it was amazing how we seemed to find each other. In one week

I saw five other cars exactly like mine. In fact, one night I pulled into the left hand turn lane at an intersection and a Porsche that looked exactly like mine pulled into the left lane across from me. It was instant brotherhood. He flashed his headlights, so I flashed mine back. He flashed them again and I flashed them back! We flashed hand fist pumps and exchanged smiles to acknowledge what we had in common and then drove away. Isn't it interesting that this Law of Attraction also holds true when it comes to belief? When you have become clear on what you believe, it is obvious that you automatically attract others who believe as you believe. Positive attracts positive – miserable being finds other miserable being, then they are happy!

The same thing holds true for someone who thinks they only deserve to drive a used car. They pull into the left hand turn lane at an intersection in their rusted out 1977 Buick with a broken muffler, a bad air shock and the two-toned paint chipping away, and sure enough, another 1977 beat up Buick pulls into the left hand turn lane facing them. Just like with a new car, it is still instantaneous brotherhood as the guy flashes you his one headlight, you flash your one headlight back, and together smile with that look, "Yo Dude, what up? Represent 'homie' – with a shout out to ya'all who don't believe you deserve the best!"

Obviously this analogy has nothing to do with socio-economic conditions. However, it does have to do with every politically correct and especially every politically incorrect scenario where a self-esteem issue is the cause of the dilemma, such as the wonderful women doing everything she knows how to do to get out of a physically and an emotionally abusive relationship, only to jump back into a more dysfunctional relationship with a bigger loser than the bum she just kicked out. Why does this happen so often? Likes attract likes. The primary goal in life should not be to get what we think we want, but to want what we get. If you don't like what you are attracting, change what's attracting it.

Bottom line. We need to crate our own personal 'Board of Directors,' which begins only when we become crystal clear on who we are and who need to continuously strive to be. Only then can we influence, inspire and attract the right people to join our team.

CHAPTER TWELVE

THE ART OF DUPLICATION & FOLLOWING THE DAN CLARK "P6" SALES SYSTEM

"I'd rather see a sermon preached than hear one any day; I'd rather you would walk with me than merely point the way."

MY FRIEND, MENTOR and colleague Hank Haney, celebrity golf instructor who coached Tiger Woods during his six best, most productive years when he won most of his Major tournaments, shared a story with me about Tiger playing in the 2008 Masters when his putting was the worst it had ever been in his life.

After winning his first three PGA Tour starts that year, Woods had now lost his past two tournaments in large part because of his putter. In the four rounds of the Masters Tiger had 28 putts Thursday, 31 on Friday and Saturday and 30 on Sunday.

That was 120 putts for the tournament, which ranked him in a tie for 29th in the field. Masters Champion Immelman, had 112 putts. After he rolled in a birdie putt on No. 18, Woods waved one of his hands in disgust, showing his disappointment with his putting. In his explanation to me about Tiger's approach to putting, Hank said Tiger simply thinks it's a good putt when it goes in, and a bad putt when he misses it. Which meant that during this Masters tournament Tiger kept tweaking his set up, changing his weight distribution, and altering his stroke every time he two or three putted a green.

In contrast, Hank has always taught that putting is a self-contained compact system, when once perfected, simply needs to be precisely duplicated on every hole with every putt. Putting is about learning the perfect putting stroke and practicing and perfectly practicing until it becomes a permanent automatic muscle-memory routine from lining up the break, grip, take away and ball striking that follows through the ball.

No, you don't change your stroke each time you miss a putt. You trust the 'system' and concentrate on making every putting stroke exactly the same from start to finish. When you do, eventually the ball will start going in the hole with great championship level regularity. Herein lies the difference between a goal and a system. The goal is to make the putt – every putt. The system is the spaced-repetition process that you've perfected over time that will allow you to achieve your goal.

Scott Adams illuminated this understanding in his book, How To Fail and Still Win Big: "A goal is a specific objective that you either achieve or don't sometime in the future. A system is something you do on a regular basis that increases your odds of happiness in the long run. If you do something every day, its a system. If you're waiting to achieve it someday in the future, it's a goal. If you achieve your goal, you celebrate and feel terrific, but only until you realize you just lost the thing that gave you purpose and direction. Your options are to feel empty and useless, perhaps enjoying the spoils of your success until they bore you, or set new goals and reenter the cycle of permanent pre-success failure.

REWARDS OF FOLLOWING
A SELLING SYSTEM

To reiterate, achieving financial success and turning it into sustained Significant Selling and Marketing high performance productivity is accomplished through the simple but powerful process of 'duplication.' When sales professionals have a specific sales system and step-by-step process that you meticulously follow, you have a 93% chance of closing the sale. Without it, your chances and closing ratios dramatically drop to 42%.

Because you now have a conviction to increase your personal and professional productivity and save time and energy in the orderly process, you are now ready to learn, understand, fully embrace, memorize and completely commit to following the most significant selling system on the planet. Welcome to:

The Dan Clark "P6" Sales System

Professional **P**erformance Skills + **P**ersuasive **P**erception Skills
x **P**ersonality **P**ositioning Skills = Significant Sales Results
(Closing Most Sales)

In the corporate world, the sports and education worlds, and even in the military construct of rank advancement, we are hired for preparation, paid for performance, but promoted on potential. Which means the one activity all worlds share is selling. And because sale's is everybody's business, let me use this most honorable profession as the classic example of why and how Significant Selling and Marketing skills and tools are used:

Our acronym **A.R.T.** is the strategic template. **"P-6" (PPPPPP)** is the tactical solution. Developing and maintaining **"Skills"** is the daily mission, with the dictionary definition of Skills being: specific proficiencies, talents, techniques, abilities and traits that are acquired and improved through training, that help you reach your full potential and set you apart from others.

Awareness: is about becoming completely literate in your "Professional Performance skills," which means you fully understand and commit to memory every fact, figure, product feature, service benefit, pricing structure and relevant piece of information required for you to do your job.

Having significant *Professional skills* means you are an expert in every one of your products and services, well educated on the most popular products and services of your top three competitors, know everything about the history of your industry, the history of your organization with its past and present leaders, and the reasons your company culture is unique and special. Because anybody can attain Professional skills, this is only the "ticket" into the game.

Having significant *Performance skills* means you have worked to be on the starting team by improving your Professional skills so you can do what you are paid to do, which gets you a better seat in the stadium.

Awareness and Professional Performance skills are the minimum requirement and entry level for being hired in an organization? Everybody with whom you work has Professional Performance skills or they wouldn't be on your team. Which means your perception is your reality.

On a scale of one to ten (1 being the worst/10 being the very best) how do you rate your Professional Performance skills, and list one thing you need to do to make each one stronger:

[   ] Your Knowledge of Every Product Feature

____

[   ] Your Knowledge of Every Service Benefit

____

[   ] Your Knowledge of Every Pricing Structure

____

[   ] Your Expertise on the Most Popular Products and Services of your Top Three Competitors

____

[   ] Your Knowledge of the History of Your Industry

____

[   ] Your Knowledge of the History of Your Organization with its Past and Present Leaders

____

[   ] Specific Reasons your Company Culture is Unique and Special

---

Because organizations pay for performance but promote based on potential, in order for you to stand out, it is critical that you continuously improve yourself by polishing your *Persuasive Perception* and perfecting your *Personality Positioning skills.*

Refinement: is about perfecting your Persuasive Perception skills," which are your sales skills. Because nobody likes to be sold, and everybody likes to buy what they want, it is critical that you learn and practice the organization's time-tested sales system until it becomes conversational so you can eloquently explain the practical application of your products and services.

Having significant *Persuasive skills* means you are an expert in the art and science of asking the right questions so you can address the prospect's pain, overcome his/her objections, and create value by eliminating the pain and providing a real solution in an understandable, meaningful way. Bottom line? You never give a "sales pitch" and always present yourself as a trusted "problem solver" and advisor to help them not only get what they want, but most significantly, want what they get so they don't die with their music still in them!

To accomplish this simple task remember that the definition of sales is the "transference of trust," I recommend the following solution:

CONVERTING 'NEEDS' TO 'WANTS' AND 'WHYS' TO 'HOW-TOS'

For decades, the most popular old school sales program was called *Needs Satisfaction Selling,* which proclaimed "the customer is king and always right," and when we identify his/her needs we can accommodate them with our product and service.

We now know this is obsolete. For example, if you live in a snow belt and NEED a vacation to get out of the cold, any tropical destination can satisfy your NEED. This is good for you, the customer, because competition among hot beach locations drives the cost down. However, low prices and a consumer's expectation to get more for less is bad for travel destinations, adventure parks and hotels that service them.

If you are taking your wife to a black tie gala and she NEEDS a new pair of black stilettos to match her gown, any brand of formal shoes can solve her dilemma.

However, if you WANT to treat your family to a two week, $25,000 vacation in Jaco, Costa Rica, or for your 25th wedding anniversary, take your sweetheart on a 30-day $30,000 exotic cruise from Fort Lauderdale, Florida to Buenos Aires, Argentina and onto Antarctica aboard a magnificent Seabourn Luxury Liner, then you'll pay these outrageous prices because the alternatives are simply below your desired results.

And if your wife WANTS a pair of $1300 Christian Louboutin *Laurence Lace Up Ankle Boots, with the French designer's* signature trademarked red-lacquered sole that can be seen from far away, that hoards of Hollywood starlets have been seen sporting at award shows, premiers and red carpet events, then the crazy and unconscionable high price is somehow acceptable and reasonable. Bottom line. If she WANTS those shoes she won't be satisfied with any alternative. In fact, the high prices actually fuel her motivation to buy them because everybody knows how much they cost!

What causes this? Brand Value. Value is always determined by what we are willing to give up in order to get it. This means the amount of money is irrelevant if the perceived value of creating a specific memory with your family that you can tell your friends about outweighs the cost; and the perceived value of purchasing a specific pair of shoe gives your wife a sense of sophisticated elegance, and the appearance that she is part of the glamorous Hollywood jet set. The desire for the brand – the WANT – is what makes the memory, product and service most valuable.

When you first move your own NEEDS to WANTS, you will understand why and how to convert the NEEDS of your associates and/or customers to WANTS. Moving NEEDS to WANTS is the quickest way to transform all WHYS to HOWS.

This means that instead of spending your time and hard-earned resources on convincing your associates and/or potential customers WHY they should follow your advice and/or buy your product and service, you can use your time and energy showing them HOW they can stay fully engaged with you and your business.

When you get people to choose YOU, not just someone who does what you do, you will find that the entire process of influence and/or sales cycle quickens and strengthens, while the HOWS become the obvious urgent next steps to reaching the mutually agreed upon desired results.

Having significant *Perception skills* means you understand the power of projecting the right "Image." From the moment you step out of your car and cross the parking lot each morning, you're a visible expression of your level of competence, confidence, where you are in your organization's culture, and where you are going in your personal life and sales career.

The way you walk, the way you sit, the clothes you wear, your language use of good grammar, please/ thank you and no vulgarity, your magnifying of the social graces, portrayal of sophisticated elegance and polished professionalism, opening the door for others, giving up your seat to the physically challenged and the elderly, and the way you treat others who are different than you, sends a strong message to your coworkers, superiors and prospective customers that "I'm prepared and ready to play the game at the highest level knowing people love to do business with a winner!"

Refinement and Persuasive Perception skills take your minimum requirement game to the competitive level where you get to play in your league and win your share of the time. Which means their perception is their reality, which is the game changer.

On a scale of one to ten (1 being the worst/10 being the very best) how do you rate your Persuasive Perception skills, and list one thing you need to do to make each one stronger:

[   ] Your Walk

____

[   ] Your Clothes/Dressing For Success and Significance

____

[   ] Your Language Use of Good Grammar, Please/ Thank You and No Vulgarity

---

[   ] Your Magnifying of the Social Graces

[   ] Portrayal of Sophisticated Elegance and Polished Professionalism

---

[   ] Opening the Door for Others, Giving Up Your Seat to the Physically Challenged and the Elderly

---

[   ] The Way You Treat Others Who Are Different Than You

Transformation: comes as you develop and continuously polish your "Personality Positioning skills," by working very hard on yourself – not by working "on" your job, but working "in" your job. Alert! Having significant *Professional Performance skills and Persuasive Perception skills* do not make you a better person. Therefore, they are never as significant as *Personality Positioning skills.*

Having significant *Personality skills* means you have *personal traits* that make you stand out in every crowd, such as being: Obedient, Fearless, Observant, Impartial, Independent, Optimistic, Intelligent, Persistent, Charming, Precise, Suave, Meticulous, and Trusting.

Having significant *Positioning skills* means you understand the short and long term ramifications of visibility, visibility, visibility. Which means you are a master networker, going out of your way to connect with coworkers and prospective customers to develop trust, mutual respect and loyalty "off task time" so on task time is more productive.

The Implementation of Dan's "P6" Sales System

Professional **P**erformance Skills + **P**ersuasive **P**erception Skills x **P**ersonality **P**ositioning Skills = Significant Sales Results

On a scale of one to ten (1 being the worst/10 being the very best) if you rate your Professional Performance skills as a 10, and add it to your Persuasive Perception skills, which is also a 10, but your Personality Positioning skills are only at a 5, when you add up the two 10s that equal 20, and multiply it by your Personality Positioning skills of 5, your calculated Significant Sales Results score is: 20 x 5 = 100.

If you rate your Professional Performance skills at only a 5, and your Persuasive Perception skills at only a 5, and your Personality Positioning skills as a 10, your Significant Sales Results score is still: 100.

However, if your Professional Performance skills are at a 10, and your Persuasive Perception skills are at a 10, AND your Personality Positioning skills are at a 10, your Significant Sales Results score jumps to 200, which gives you the competitive advantage at home, school, work and play.

The true accelerator and significant multiplier in closing sales (anybody can make a presentation); and the significant accelerator and true multiplier in creating an extraordinary customer experience (resulting in customer service delight and referrals), is the continuous dedication to developing and enhancing your Personality Positioning Skills.

Transformation and Personality Positioning skills maximize your potential and give you the competitive advantage to compete out of your league at the highest world class level so you dominate your competition in every game/market and win every contract.

According to the Carnegie Institute of Technology, *85% of your financial success is due to your personality and ability to communicate, negotiate and lead.* On a scale of 1 to 10 (1 weakest/10 strongest), rate your proficiency in Twenty-Four Personality Positioning Skills and circle the ones on which you need to improve:

TWENTY-FOUR PERSONALITY POSITIONING SKILLS

[   ] Positive: Genuinely Enthusiastic

[   ] Confident: Humble yet Fully Assured/High Self Worth

[   ] Courageous: The Ability to Do What's Right in the Toughest Situations

---

[   ] Conscientious: Good Moral Understanding of Right and Wrong

---

[   ] Consistent: Demonstrating the same Attitude, Integrity, Character, and Commitment to Excellence at all times, in all places, on and off task

---

[   ] Sophisticated: Master of the Social Graces – Polite – Gracious – Thankful – Thoughtful – Strong But Gentle – Empathetic – Kind

---

[   ] Social: The Desire to Be with People and the Ability to Work with Them

---

[   ] Well-Read: The Ability to Carry On a Conversation about many varying topics in the Seven Fields of Knowledge – History, Literature, Visual Arts, Science, Music, Philosophy and Religion

---

[   ] Interested: The Ability to Get Others to Talk About Themselves

---

[   ] Present: The Ability to Be 'In The Moment' and Intently Listen

---

[   ] Driven: The Capacity to be a Self-Starter

[   ] Directed: The Ability to Set Clearly Defined Goals

[   ] Responsible: The Ability to Take Full Responsibility for every Positive/Negative Action

---

[   ] Mentally Tough: The Capacity to Handle Rejection

[   ] Adaptable: The Capacity to Handle Sudden Change/Agile/Nimble

---

[   ] Calm: The Capacity to Think and Perform Under Pressure

[   ] Resilient: The Capacity to Cope, and turn each Stumbling Block into a Stepping Stone and every Set Back into a Comeback

---

[   ] Resourceful: Knowing there is Always a Way – It's Just Finding It

---

[   ] Organized: Efficient Attention to Detail

[   ] Hard Working: Intolerant of Minimum Requirement Effort and Mediocre Performance

---

[   ] Reliable: Trustworthy/Dependable/Conscientious

[   ] Articulate: Extraordinary Verbal Skills as a Master Communicator of the Art and Science of Persuasion

---

[   ] Elegant: Extraordinary Non-Verbal Skills Showcasing your Eye Contact, Firm Hand Shake, Smile, Hair, Polished Shoes, Significant Attire

---

[   ] Visible: Highly Involved in Charitable Causes/Volunteering in Schools, Parks, Clubs, Community Events

---

PAID FOR PERFORMANCE / PROMOTED ON POTENTIAL

Remember, traditional companies pay for performance, but they promote on potential. Which means Awareness and Professional skills are the minimum requirement and entry level for being hired in a traditional organization. Everybody with whom you work has professional skills, or they wouldn't be on your team. And because this is only the minimum entry-level requirement, it only buys you a ticket into the stadium to play. These are NOT the people you want to attract and recruit into your Direct Sales/Network Marketing organization. They come and go and end up taking way too much of your time.

Refinement and Persuasive skills take your minimum requirement game to the competitive level where you get to play in your league and win your share of the time.

Transformation and Personality skills maximize your potential and give you the competitive advantage to compete out of your league at the highest world class level so you dominate your competition in every game/market and win every contract.

Bottom line. Obedience to this simple, powerful formula called "P-6" is not only the *secret sauce* to becoming a consummate sales professional, but it is the alga rhythm that prepares and positions you to be promoted to the most significant leadership roles and responsibilities in your organization.

ALWAYS APPEAL TO ONE'S SENSE OF HUMANITY

The only place from which people can grow is where they are. We must go where they are physically, mentally and emotionally. Only there can we gently invite them to improve and buy. Therefore, **in** the volatile world of selling, the transformational process from going from a successful entry level 'Distributor' to a Significant Network Marketing Sales and Organizational Development Champion begins when you tap into the humanity of your prospect, which means you connect with them as total persons – packaging your logical case so that it touches their feelings, needs, and values.

Everything you say has the potential to trigger some sort of emotional response in your prospect. You can strengthen your 'Close' by selecting main points, supporting material, and language that can engage your prospect's feelings.

Positive emotions like delight, pride and love are surefire motivators, especially when you exceed their expectations. When used properly, negative emotions like fear, anger, disgust, and contempt can also motivate as in roller coasters and horror films. It all depends on the needs of your prospect.

For example, because you are selling 'Life Unlimited,' by first asking questions about their personal health including their level of energy and desired level of fitness; and inquiring about their current family situation; and wondering if they have an entrepreneurial bug to want to own, build and run their own million dollar business that can also employ their children and friends as they help them become fellow millionaires; and asking about their individual concerns with their bodies, skincare, ailments and diseases; and inquiring about their level of personal development and leadership training, you could appeal to your prospect at any of the following levels:

The effect of nutritional supplements coupled with exercise in a weight loss or weight management program, showing them why and how it reduces the risk of cardiovascular disease, diabetes, and obesity, which appeals to their survival need.

- The issue of security might also be drawn in by mentioning how physically fit people are more likely to be able to resist or evade attackers.

- The need for belonging can be linked to becoming trim and attractive, as well as to making friends through physical activity.

- Esteem needs can be tied into the current popularity of fitness and the social desirability of an active image.

- And, fitness can be related to the need for self-actualization – the highs of exercise, and the mental and physical challenge of reaching one's potential.

The effect of Essential Oils in healing certain sicknesses, relieving pain and soreness, clearing up allergies, sinus congestion, and headaches, trimming and toning their bodies in skinny dipping baths, or simply relaxing their minds, bodies and souls at the end of a long stressful work day.

The effect of an active lifestyle full of quality relationships, inquiring if they have enough family time together and what and when was the last major vacation they shared, and would it be important if they could figure out a way to make more money and free up more time to create more quality and quantity family togetherness?

Bottom line. This sales cycle is officially called the 'Sales Process,' which is an intimate exercise in diagnosing a customers needs by asking the right questions and listening. And because you took the necessary time to authentically connect with the prospect at the 'needs' based, intellectual facts, features and benefits level, and turn their needs into passionate personal 'want's at the emotional relationship level; and because 'the sale does not begin until the customer says no;' and because a person's decision to buy is made during this diagnosis 'process' where price is never mentioned and competition is never present, the prospect doesn't feel they are being sold, and looks at you as a trusted advisor whom they will tell on their time frame when they are ready to buy.

For these reasons, 85 percent of all sales take place *after* the fourth sales call, which means it is critical that you do enough homework on your prospect before this process begins, so you can formulate and put in place a calculated four-encounter plan that progressively builds trust, loyalty, friendship, mutual respect and support by the fifth sales call, which is really the only true sales call because the previous four interactions were considered the "process."

When you have carefully and successfully transformed their perception of you from "Expected Credibility" (you know only as much as they do) to "Phenomenal Expert," where you know, understand and have experienced more than they have and can honestly advise them with no bias on what and why they should buy, it is time to tactfully and gracefully transition from the sales process into your well-prepared persuasive official 'Sales Presentation.'

Six Key Cautions For Your Sales Presentation

- Prior to the start of this 'Closing,' make sure you have in place a non-threatening, low/no pressure decision-making process. In the absence of a quality decision-making process the decision degrades and disintegrates to the lowest common denominator, which is always price. If price becomes the topic of conversation it means the presentation is weak and the relationship is non-existent.

- Don't misuse your allotted time and overstay your welcome. You must show up early and leave exactly when you said you would. Too many go into an appointment and "shoot the breeze" and then need to impose and go overtime to close the sale.

- Don't be too informative. It's boring. Be more persuasive, more emotional. Help them answer "why" so they can figure out that their "how to" is the solution you provide!

- Don't wear the wrong thing. No matter what you have worn during the four encounters during the sales "process," when you schedule the fifth and formal sales "presentation," it is critical for men to wear a coat and tie and women to be dressed to a professional tee. Psychologically this says you are a serious, well prepared, polished professional whom they should do business with right now!

- Don't "wing it." The shorter the appointment time slot the more prepared and calculated you must be!

- Don't be a weak or lousy presenter. The greatest skill a sales pro or leader can develop is the ability to deliver a polished persuasive presentation!

Chapter Thirteen

The Art
Of Perseverance

"The Sale Doesn't Begin Until The Customer Says 'No'"

ONE DAY WHILE sitting by a stream, a man noticed a steady trickle of water hitting a rock. It was only a drip, but it was constant—drop after drop after drop. He found it fascinating that a hole had been carved out by that steady drip of water.

How could that be? The man concluded that if something as soft as water can carve a hole in solid rock, how much more so the constant flow of provocative thoughts and powerful words make an indelible impression on our hearts and actions.

Think about this. Every drop of knowledge and wisdom—and every time we obey even the seemingly insignificant rules—makes an impact with unparalleled power to effect change. Sometimes we do not perceive it, and the results are not apparent until years later. But if we keep at it, the power of perseverance, drop after drop after drop, continuously carves and penetrates us forever.

Achieving significance comes not so much through dramatic bursts of insight and inspiration. Experiences are fleeting; once they end, the connection quickly dissipates. Rather, it is the consistent striving to live the Twelve Highest Universal Laws taught in my best-selling book The Art of Significance – Achieving The Level Beyond Success, the small triumphs of the soul—that adds drop after drop to ultimately create a true physical, mental, emotional, spiritual, and financial transformation from success to significance.

Why Persevere?

One of the very best examples of perseverance in the business world is my friend David Buckwald, an outstanding husband and father and an extremely successful insurance sales professional and financial services adviser working out of New Jersey. When you talk to him, he is extremely proud of what he does for a living and the number of families he has been able to help take care of over the years.

Truly, David had answered why he chose his insurance profession and was enjoying the lifestyle it afforded him and his beautiful wife and young family. Then, one day forever changed his perspective and reasons to persevere.

The day was September 11, 2001. For reasons most of us do not fully understand, the Twin Towers of the World Trade Center in New York City were attacked. Nearly three thousand innocent lives were lost. Among the dead were fifty-one of David's clients whom he considered friends. Within a few days after the heroic rescue had been completed and tragically turned into a sad and painful recovery, David delivered fifty-one death-benefit checks to the heartbroken widows left behind.

On more than one occasion, I have shared the platform with David and has heard him speak to fellow insurance and financial products professionals about his experience and how and why he is so glad that he never took "no" for an answer from his prospective clients.

David persevered because he knew what a generous insurance policy would mean to a man's family if for some reason his life was taken early. Therefore, David was relentless in calling back time and time again until he was granted an appointment so he could share what he was so proud to sell. Thank heaven David knew that the sale does not begin until the customer says "no."

That is not the end of his story. Two weeks after he had attended the last of the fifty-one funerals, David ironically received two phone calls on the same afternoon from two other widows explaining that as they were going through their deceased husbands' things, they each had found a $2 million dollar insurance policy and wanted to know what the status of the policy was. As he investigated their requests, David sadly discovered that both men had stopped paying the premiums six months before. There was nothing he could do to reinstate the coverage.

Patience Is Not A Virtue

We've all been taught that Patience is a virtue. Not always. Any virtue taken to the extreme can become a vice. Patience allows us to never begin. Patience invites us to mindlessly wait our turn, believing this is the hand I've been dealt, this is the cross I must bear, and everything that happens to me is meant to be. No! We must commit to 'persevere.' Perseverance is patience with a purpose, where we proactively take our turn because we know why we should.

In sales:

44% of sales professional quit after the first sales call;
24% quit after the second sales call;
14% quit after the third call;
12% quit after the fourth call.

That's 94% of sales professionals quit by the fourth sales call. Yet statistics show that 85% of sales are closed between the fifth and the twelfth sales calls.

The Significant Fifth

For these reasons, 85 percent of all sales take place *after* the fourth sales call, which means it is critical that you do enough homework on your prospect before this process begins, so you can formulate and put in place a calculated four-encounter plan that progressively builds trust, loyalty, friendship, mutual respect and support by the fifth sales call, which is really the only true sales call because the previous four interactions were considered the "process."

This means the fifth sales call is when you dress up, schedule an official office visit with a previously and clearly stated intention that you are coming by to answer the prospects final questions, enroll them in your business, give them some product, pick up a check and close the deal with signatures.

Conclusive lesson? We better make ourselves so interesting, compelling to be around and fascinating to talk to that prospective customers will want to invite us into their space as many times as is required to close the deal because we always part saying, "I like me best when I'm with you, I want to see you gain!"

When it comes to perfecting the Art of Significant Selling, Marketing and Closing More Deals, most important of all is your relentless commitment to persevere. No one in the world can expect to start a business and be profitable within the first 120 days. No one! To experience initial sales and financial success, which then turns into sustained organizational and financial growth, begins with a positive attitude and a relentless commitment to stay focused and work hard for a minimum of 120 days, by listening to and meticulously following a leader who has already done and continues to do what you dream to do. The guarantee in becoming a Significant Sales and Marketing Professional is that perseverance always pays off!

The goal is to simply go as far as you can see, and that doesn't have to be that far. You don't need to see the top of the staircase before you start to climb. You don't have to see New York City to begin your journey in Los Angeles. You need only get on the right road and turn on your light.

To illustrate: the headlight on my Harley Davidson motorcycle projects 100 feet in front of the bike. Which means that on any day, in any weather condition, in the sunlight and especially in the dark, I can get from where I am to anywhere I want to go 100 feet at a time. And because the headlight continuously projects 100 feet ahead, the key is to start our journey and to keep going.

Bottom line. The possibilities are endless, but only when you Persevere. Proof?

APPLE APATHY

Ronald Wayne was 25 years old, working with Steve Jobs at Atari before he, Jobs, and Wozniak founded Apple Computer on April 1, 1976. Serving as the venture's "adult supervision", Wayne drew the first Apple Logo, wrote the three men's original Partnership Agreement, and wrote the operating Owners Manual for the new Apple 1 computer.

In the Agreement Wayne received a 10% stake in Apple, but because all members of a partnership are personally responsible for any debts incurred by any partner; and because Wayne was still licking his wounds from a failed company that he had started five years earlier, Wayne relinquished his equity for US$800 less than two weeks later, on April 12, 1976. Later that year, venture capitalist Arthur Rock helped Jobs and Wozniak develop a business plan that converted Apple to a corporation. A year after leaving Apple, Wayne received $1,500 for his agreement to forfeit any claims against the new company.

In its first year of operations (1976), Apple's sales reached $174,000. Sales rose to $2.7 million in 1977, to $7.8 million in 1978, and to $117 million in 1980. In February 2015, Apple's value exceeded $700 billion. Had Wayne kept his 10% stock and 'persevered' until then, it would now be worth approximately $60 billion.

Chapter Fourteen
The Art Of Closing More Sales

"The sale doesn't begin until the customer says 'no.'"

—Zig Ziglar

In my experience, if money becomes the topic of conversation it means the presentation was weak, the relationship is non-existent, and the closing conversation was even weaker.

If at the end of your presentation the price is still too high, you ask one more question: 'Are you concerned more about the price or the cost?' To which most respond, 'What's the difference?' Which opens up the opportunity for you to pull out a pen and paper to give your explanation. Why? Because we've been conditioned to believe what we see and doubt what we hear, seeing spawns logic, hearing creates emotion. When you combine the two it increases your chances of closing the sale.

Identify And Measure Price Against Cost

Every Universal Law has a "price" we can choose to pay through obedience, which guarantees we will reap the specific reward attached to that law; or a "cost" we can choose to pay through disobedience, which guarantees we will suffer the specific consequence attached to that law.

In a TV commercial, an auto mechanic, who is explaining to his customer that he can either pay a small sum now for an oil change and an oil filter or pay a far larger sum later for a new engine states, "Pay me now, or pay me later."

No baby is destined at birth to become a criminal. The road to criminal behavior is paved with childhood abuse and neglect, inadequate preparation for school, unaddressed behavior problems, poor academic performance, and dropping out of high school.

The "price" to develop the physical, intellectual, emotional, and social well-being of a child is calculated to be approximately $12,401 per student per year, which is driven by school readiness, the ability to respect authority and get along with others, parental involvement in academic achievement, wholesome after-school programs, and high school graduation.

The "cost" to incarcerate one person in prison per year is between $31,000 and $60,076, depending on the state. Pay for it now, or pay for it later.

> It's better to build a fence at the edge of a cliff than to park an ambulance at its base.

The difference between price and cost is discovered when a dad takes his son to the Schwinn shop to buy him a new bike. The price tag is $100, so the dad goes to a discount store, where a salesman convinces him to buy a cheaply made bike for only $50.

Two weeks later the seat wiggles loose from the frame and needs to be repaired. Because there is no warranty, the dad is charged $20 for the repair. Two weeks later the handlebars bend down, and two weeks after that the bearings in the back wheel freeze up and the chain breaks, forcing the dad back to the store to pay another $60 in repairs.

Dad complains, scolding the owner for selling him a lemon, angrily pays the bill, and storms out! (In reality it was his fault for letting someone influence him to make a poor choice!)

When the other wheel seizes up, dad throws the bike in the trash and buys the Schwinn he should have purchased in the first place. Although the "price" of the cheap bike was only $50, in just six weeks the "cost" of that bike had risen to $130! The price of the Schwinn was

$100, but because it was well built, the son ended up riding it for ten years with no additional cost.

Bottom line: Price is a one-time thing—paying the price of obedience to a law always creates a controlled, positive result. Cost is a lifetime thing - paying the cost of disobedience to a law always creates an uncontrolled negative result. In both cases there are no surprises. Will you pay the price now and enjoy the prize forever, or will you pay the cost now and suffer the consequence forever? The choice is always there and always yours.

Bottom line. The 'price' of the Schwinn was considerably more than the poorly made bike. But the 'cost' of the cheaper bike was considerably higher. So in this 'close' you again ask and then point out to your prospect:

"So, again I ask you (Mr./Ms. Prospect), is it the price or the cost you are concerned with? I know a lot of companies and their sales professionals can beat me on price, but I guarantee nobody can beat me and my company on cost! And because price is a one-time thing, and cost is a lifetime thing, don't you really want the best possible, lowest cost?" Now simply smile and have him/her sign the contract!

Chapter Fifteen

The Art And Benefits Of Following Time-Tested Systems

Achieving initial sales success and turning it into sustained Significant financial and client base growth is accomplished through the simple but powerful process of 'duplication.'

We have all heard, 'Proper Prior Planning Prevents Poor Performance;' 'If you don't know where you're going it doesn't matter what bus you take;' 'When you keep doing what you did you'll keep getting what you got;' 'Insanity is believing you can keep doing the same thing and expect a different result." Hmmm. What do these clichés mean to you? To me, they point out the six major elements of the significance of 'planning your work and working your plan, which in turn is what always gives you the 'Competitive Advantage.'

Five Elements To Creating Competitive Advantage

One:

You should create your own personal 'Board of Directors' who are at your disposal for a phone call 24/7 or open for a meeting on a moments notice, who prove true that you may win a few games with the 'best players,' but you can only win the championship with the 'right people.' Select significant individuals whom you love and respect and connect with at every level of life because they inspire you to reach your full potential in your physical, mental, spiritual, emotional, social, financial, familial, recreational, and charitable giving aspects of living. The list of unique qualities found in 'right people' is best described by my friend, colleague and former super star coach Chris Estes as 'Five Star Recruits,' which means they qualify under five major attributes he calls his 'differentiating factors,' that also refer and attract the right 'Five Star People" into your organization:

FIVE STAR RECRUITS

1. **Desire** – I want someone who wants something more than what they currently have and be something more;

2. **Coachable** – humble enough so they are teachable, moldable, not 'choke-able!'

3. **Influence** – wanting to always add value to everybody they meet;

4. **A Winner** – with a track record of previous successes;

5. **Personality** – that is inviting, contagious, energetic, and positive, knowing it's your 'flavor that creates

TWO:

You obviously have to engage in my simple but profound:

THE PROVEN PROCESS
OF GOAL SETTING

1. Replace your old school beliefs that 'It's not over until it's over,' and 'It's not over until the fat lady sings,' with the firm conviction, 'It's Not Over 'Til I Win!'

2. Dream a mighty dream (if you don't have a dream, how are you going to make a dream come true. When you lose your dream you die. That's why we have so many people walking the halls of life who are dead and they don't even know it!

3. Turn your dream into a specific goal by writing it down.

4. Make the goal big and important with long-range ramifications so exciting that it inspires you to persevere through the short-term frustrations.

5. Give yourself a specific time limit.

6. List your obstacles that you must face, effectively deal with and efficiently overcome so you can continue to move forward. (A big goal also includes a one-week goal and even an important one-day goal, and how we deal with all the obstacles and details required on a minute-by-minute, hour-by-hour basis.)

7. Identify the people and resources that will be required to help you deal with your obstacles and turn your dream into a goal and your goal into a reality. Obviously this list must also include phone numbers and email addresses so you can immediately contact them to get your teamwork under way.

To illustrate: A good friend phones you at 10:30 am on Monday morning with an offer you can't refuse. He invites you and your significant other to come with him and his wife to Cancun, Mexico for the next seven days, all expenses paid, at an exclusive five star resort, with golf, zip-lining, historic tours, white water rafting, swimming with the dolphins and more. It won't cost you a dime! The only challenge is that you are leaving the next morning at 10:30 am. Will you say 'yes?' Of course you would – we all would!

Excitedly you hang up the phone, but as you start sharing the news with your significant other, reality sets in and you sadly remember five things you have to do in the next week. With a somber gulp you interrupt yourself and blurt, "What a drag! We can't go to Mexico. I've got too much to do. There is no way!"

To which your significant other interrupts you, "Of course there is a way! There is always a 'way!' We just need to find it! We are not letting this $10,000 dollar vacation slip away without a fight!" And he/she proceeds to interview you and itemize the five things you need to accomplish, which triggers an influx of passion, imagination and creativity to help you resolve each of them. Not surprising to him/her, the two of you depart on time the next morning at 10:30 to join your friends on this phenomenal and free holiday adventure!

Question: How much could you get accomplished in your life if you approached every day as if you were leaving for Cancun the next morning? When your 'why' is bigger and more important than your 'why not,' it's amazing what we will get accomplished in a short period of time. Although we didn't itemize the details of how the couple rose to the occasion to join their friends on the Cancun holiday, it is obvious that our previously itemized seven steps to goal setting were followed in sequential order and with zeal!

Three:

There are systems and models for every discipline and endeavor. My friend and colleague, Bob Pike, one of the elite trainers of trainers, trusted advisers, and premier success coaches on the planet, teaches a personal development system to blend facts with inspiring feelings:

K + M = PP Knowledge plus motivation equals peak performance.

K – M = LEI Knowledge minus motivation equals
less-than-expected improvement.

M – K = EI Motivation minus knowledge equals
energized incompetence.

Notice that knowledge minus motivation *disappoints* and that motivation minus knowledge *breeds mediocrity*. As Mr. Miyagi counseled in the movie *Karate Kid,* "Ambition without knowledge is like a boat on dry land." Obviously, succeeding at anything, and then taking that success to the highest level of performance requires an equal measure of motivation and knowledge. One without the other is a waste.

Four:

There is a specific time-tested formula for starting your own business. Because the remuneration for services of a sales professionals is one of three compensation plans: Base Salary, Base plus Bonus, or

Base plus Commission, every professional sales person is a consummate entrepreneur. Therefore, I present to you the definitive process on entrepreneurship developed and proven true by my friend and colleague, Dr. Michael Glauser, PhD., international business strategy consultant, best selling author, former Professor/Director of the Institute For New Enterprise at Westminster College, (SLC, Utah; and former Director of Free Enterprise Education at Huntsman School of Business, Utah State University. Dr. Glauser teaches a system he calls:

The Fundamental Principles of Entrepreneurship

- **Live on the Edge:** (preparation) Effective businesses start where costumers meet.

- **Plan for opportunities:** (continually prepare) Find new costumers. Look for opportunities, look for a need.

- **Engage Helpful Mentors:** (partner) They will help you.

- **Build Powerful Teams:** (develop synergy) Create loyal partnerships with vendors and suppliers.

- **Work with Zeal-Acity:** (perform) Have a passion for products.

- **Get More for Less:** (cinch up the belt) Go in Lean – Stay Lean.

- **Offer Mind-Boggling Service:** (work on purpose) Exceed customer expectations.

- **Serve a Broader Purpose:** (have a visible cause-marketing campaign). The business must support the community.

Remember: a 'significant' sales system is not about providing standard stock answers. It's always about asking the right questions. So again I remind you – we need to be crystal clear on who we are and who need to continuously strive to be, so we can influence and inspire others to join our team where they can find the necessary support required to do the same.

Five:

The following is a quick checklist of fundamental things that all sales professionals need to do, regardless of your industry or the product and service you sell, regardless if you are a beginning rookie or a seasoned vet – especially when the market tightens up and recessionary times get us down. I call it:

The Dozen Do's of Networking and Staying Connected

1. As in the world of real estate sales, the Art of Significant Selling, Marketing and Closing More Deals is also about 'location, location, location' – but not of property, of yourself. Networking your way in to an authentically 'connected' relationship is about 'Visibility, Visibility, Visibility!' You must be visible at your community schools, sporting and arts events, and special occasions. It's volunteer, volunteer, volunteer, get involved, make a difference, give more than you take! Whenever the economy goes into a recession, we must beware that the first six letters of recession are "recess." In most down markets, a majority of commissioned sales people lose intensity and relax thinking everybody else is slacking off and struggling so this is a good time for me to do the same and take my well deserved "recess." No! True sales professionals always use a slow economy to better position themselves as a mover and shaker in the community, getting involved in charity events and taking advantage of opportunities to meet leaders in other fields and develop relationships with potential clients who are currently with a competitor.

2. Create a wall chart grid set up with a specific time management daily and weekly calendar based on fixed and variable slots (musts and wants), displaying a month to month / year to year running total of where you are with specific physical health goals (exercise, sleeping, eating), mental goals (reading, product knowledge, foreign language study, general education), and financial goals (how you are exceeding company quotas so you qualify for every sales

bonus and incentive trip offered!) The day grid is Sunday through Saturday and should be filled out in detail so you can actually see and track your progress, "scratch where it itches" so you can adjust your strategy before it's too late, and get your desired result.

3. Itemize this calendar grid chart into planning time, preparation time, prospecting time, sales processing time, and presentation time knowing the average number of presentations you must make before you close a sale is between five and twelve. Set only one goal in each area at a time, focusing on what you can control and letting go of what you can't.

4. At the end of your sales process (how ever long it took) which culminates in your official sales presentation where you dress up, schedule an official office visit, ask for the sale and close the deal with signatures, make sure you have in place a great, non-threatening, low/no pressure decision-making process. In the absence of a quality decision-making process, the decision degrades and disintegrates to the lowest common denominator, which is always price. Because nobody wants to be "sold," the goal is to get them to "buy," and the decision to buy is made in the "diagnosis" where price is never mentioned and competition is never present. Diagnosing a customers needs is an intimate exercise in asking the right questions and listening. Then and only then can you take their perception of you from "Expected Credibility" (you know only as much as they do) to "Phenomenal Credibility" (you know, understand and have experienced more than they have and can honestly advise them with no bias on what and why they should buy!)

5. Always fill out all of the paperwork in this presentation meeting and definitely get the check for payment in full then and there before you leave. "Buyers Remorse" is a real phenomenon. To circumvent it from derailing the sale, entertain a question and answer session addressing both their major complaints and minor objections before you start your close. Then go for it, totally unashamed and unafraid to help them get what they need, want and desire!

6. Ask for the names, physical addresses, and email addresses of five of this new clients friends and fellow businessmen and women whom they believe would benefit from your program, products and ser-

vices. Get this client to personally phone the customer (even if he is in the hospital) and encourage him to set up an appointment with you where you can explain your point of view, products, services, processes, and system of success.

7. Be an expert in your field. In the case of Real Estate sales, my Realtor (who is awesome, very successful, and happens to be my beautiful sister Debbie), taught me that a Realtor needs to become ones real estate agent long before we need him/her to help us buy or sell a property. Debbie taught me about "sellers" and "buyers" markets and the whys of a self-correcting market by asking, "Who owns your equity? The bank? You? No. The market does. You don't have any money in your hand until you sell the property. The market holds it until you sell, and the price is only what the market will bear.

8. Be brilliant at the basics. Investigate and compare the specific thoughts, steps, procedures and behaviors that extremely successful and significant sales professionals use in their diverse industries and figure out how to apply them to your world. What has made my amazing, successful and significant sister Debbie a perennial sales champion realtor, is that regardless of how successful and busy she is, or how tough the market is, she continues to do what each of us need to continuously do:

9. Phone twenty friends, acquaintances and referrals daily to let them know you are thinking about them and available to help in any way. Research so you can mention something about their personal lives. Follow up the call by sending the twenty individuals corresponding personal handwritten 'Notes' simply stating that you 'appreciate knowing them' or 'their amazing reputation precedes them, and that you look forward to getting to know them.'

10. Compile and always keep updated your comprehensive personal mailing list accumulated from parties, receptions, weddings, graduations, etc., and add it to your Facebook friends and Twitter followers (whenever you can get their physical mailing addresses) – and especially everyone on your email list, and SEND a personal Quarterly Newsletter outlining your goals for the forthcoming months. Included in the newsletter should be an intimate

personal experience, a powerful inspirational story, a hilarious quote, your forecast for your industry, and a thank you for their friendship and support, again asking them for referrals and their continued support.

11. Identify the most powerful and influential individuals in your area, and make sure each of them receives a unique and beautiful calendar every holiday season – one that is artistic and posh enough to hang up, which keeps your name ever present before them. This calendar should also be sent to your competing sales professionals, local and state politicians, school board members, Superintendents and building Principals, and to the powerful small business owners and key decision makers in your area, with an accompanying note stating that their influence on your community matters to you.

12. Even in politics we need to use our influence to help make our country everything it needs to be and has the power to become. Therefore, invest 30 minutes to contact (by letter, phone, email, and personal office visit if possible) an elected official six times each and every year. This will make you more active than 99.9% of all US citizens and therefore, 99.9% more legislatively successful.

CHAPTER SIXTEEN
THE ART OF INFLUENCE

"It is not enough to say 'I will do my best.' We must succeed in doing that which is necessary. Necessary is focusing on W.I.N. – What's Important Now."

ONE THING ALL human beings have in common is that sale's is everybody's business, which means customer service is not a department – it's a philosophical way of life. Regardless if we are focused on attracting the right people to become our friends, courting someone to marry (and especially doing what is required on a daily basis to stay married), being a good neighbor, getting the job of our dreams, or actually working as a sales professional to create extraordinary customer experiences, we are all engaged in the Art of Influencing each other.

Because the sale does not begin until the customer says 'no,' the fundamental definition of sales is the 'transference of trust.' Which validates the words of my friend and colleague Simon Sinek, "The goal is not to engage and do business with everybody who wants what you have. The goal is to engage and do business only with those who believe what you believe – so people, employers, customers, coaches, fellow players, coworkers and friends choose you, not just somebody who does what you do."

So, the questions are: "Who are you – really? Why should I choose to associate and do business with you? Are you everything you were born to be – the best you can possibly be? You'll make a lousy somebody else! Or, are you caught in a funk because the people you have been hanging out with have negatively influenced you into being somebody you are not?

From a sales perspective, what makes someone extraordinary so people choose you instead of just someone who does what you do? It's our commitment to live our lives on a higher plane that inspires others to do the same, so whenever we part ways they say, 'I like me best when I'm with you, I want to see you again.' Not just feeling good, but believing they can actually overcome their limiting beliefs, take themselves to the next level and live the life of significance that you are exemplifying.

For these reasons, in order for an audience member to open up his/her mind and heart, truly listen to what the presenter is sharing, and unconditionally trust the facts and feelings they are experiencing, each of us seeks and must find the answers to three categorical questions. Regardless if it is one person riding in the car of a realtor, a couple or small business group listening to the presentation of a Financial Advisor, or one of several thousand attendees at a huge convention, each of us seeks and must find the answers to three questions. I call it the:

"SPEAKERS TRIANGLE"

CREDIBILTY

WHY SHOULD I LISTEN TO YOU?
My history? My current situation?

POSSIBILITY

CAN I DO IT TOO?
With my weaknesses?
With my limitations?
With my strengths?

USABILITY

WHAT DO I DO NEXT?
How do I get from where I am to where I want to be?
Teach me The System – Give me the Action Plan

In every conversation, when you answer, "Why should I listen to you? Can I do it too? and What do I do next? you become an 'artist of influence,' giving assurance to them that they can trust you, follow your example, listen to your proposed solutions to their challenges, and accept your counsel and advice.

Remember: nobody likes to be sold. But everybody likes to buy and do business with a winner who has done it, and is currently doing it with his/her weaknesses and strengths.

The Eight Principles And Methods Of Significant Influence

Have you ever bought candy from a child you don't know, or purchased something from late night television that you didn't need, or subscribed to a magazine you will never read, or gone out of your way to fit something into your already crammed schedule? Specific techniques were used to get us to say yes! Itemizing these principles and methods and becoming familiar with the how, why, when, and where they can be most effectively used, will not only help us defend ourselves against future requests, but when it is our turn to persuade others to buy what we are selling, (there is no such thing as a financial crisis, only an idea crisis, ideas create income), and it is our responsibility for others to learn what we are teaching and to follow where we are leading, we will be fluent in the Eight Principles and Methods of Significant Influence.

1. Create Value and Flow

Wealth flows through you, not to you. You can get anything in life you want if you are willing to help enough other people get what they want. Significant Sellers, Marketers and Closers are inspirational "connectors and conduits" who take others from helplessness to hopefulness, building a bridge from fear to faith by providing opportunities for personal growth and increased organizational productivity for anyone who is "Willing to Win!"

2. Ask The Right Questions

If you think about it, you cannot, not answer a question. Questions create immediate involvement. Out of the Twelve Influencers in your toolbox, Questioning is the most often used by Master Persuaders. Skilled negotiators ask more than twice as many questions as average negotiators. Questions elicit an automatic response from our brains. Even if we don't verbalize the answer, we think of a response every time we are asked a question. He or she who asks the questions is in complete control of the conversation. You can get wrong answers from negative questions and you can get wrong answers from right questions, but you cannot get right answers from the wrong questions. Life is not about answers; it's about questions. If you really analyze it, life is nothing more than just a string of back-to-back questions linked together, fueled by our curiosity and commitment to uncover the whole truth. Only when we ask the right questions can we get the right answers and progress to the next right question.

3. Live By Psychological Reciprocity

A person repays what another person has provided; a sense of future obligation, which perpetuates relationships. In a conversation, if you make someone feel intelligent, important, creative, respected and powerful, it automatically creates a subconscious moral obligation in that someone to reciprocate and make you feel equally intelligent, important, creative, respected and powerful before the conversation ends. What goes around comes back around. The Adage, "one good turn deserves another" appears to be a part of every circumstance.

For example, when a man presents a woman with flowers, takes her out to a movie and afterwards treats her to an elegant dinner with expensive drinks at a posh country club, although she is flattered and enjoys the high end evening, she feels an uncomfortable sense of obligation to repay her male companion. And worse, she is more frustrated by the perception held by the suitor that, because of how much money he has spent on her, the woman would or should be more forth coming with her feelings and intimate affection. This law of obligation can also be used to eliminate suspicion, hurt, humiliation and anger. Whenever we say or do something that offends or hurts someone, regardless if it was intentional or not, buying that person a gift or suddenly going the extra mile in providing them exceptional service as part of your apology works wonders to turn the negative feelings and situation into a positive.

Every Christmas at least one person we didn't count on unexpectedly delivers a present to our home. The pressure to reciprocate and give them a gift is so strong ("Oh thank you. We are delivering our gifts later on this evening and I'll drop yours off in a while" – Yea right! Who are we fooling?) that even though we didn't have a gift for them and would never have taken them one if they had not brought us one, simply because they did this for us, we feel morally and ethically compelled to do the same for them before the day is through. Failure to reciprocate is universally viewed with contempt as being selfish, self-centered and disgusting. Even tightwads feel the influence of reciprocation as in the guy who walks into the restaurant and tells the maître d', "I'm a terrible tipper so I'd like a lousy waitress so I won't feel guilty."

4. Utilize Popular Proof

Strength in numbers. People decide what to believe and how to act in a situation based on what other people are believing and doing there. Social Proof is especially effective when people are uncertain and look to the actions of the majority to guide their own actions. It's the dancer or cheerleader who can't remember all the choreography and looks to the girl in front or to the side of her to follow her moves. It's wanting to be stylish and dressing only in the brand name clothing fads gracing the bodies of celebs.

It's advertisers and marketers knowing that babies and puppies automatically stimulate an association with warmth, trust, innocence and cuddly in the minds of their potential customers. Consequently, we see automobile commercials with puppy dogs and tire commercials with babies, even though tires and cars are not warm and cuddly. These emotional appeals create positive associations with the human element, family safety and relational side of these products in our mind. Consider the advertising tag lines, "Think Outside The Bun," "Are You In Good Hands?" "Finger Lickin Good," and "The Breakfast of Champions." Using slogans in this way allowed Taco Bell, All State,

Kentucky Fried Chicken and Wheaties to create positive feelings and binding associations without having to create a new image, and by so doing, these marketers used Social Proof in a different way to attract potential customers to go along.

In the 1960's, a cigarette company used a tag line slogan to make smoking glamorous, "Winston tastes good like a cigarette should." And let's not forget, "It's Miller Time," with it's accompanying competition chant staged at a popular bar, where one side yells "Tastes Great" and the other side yells back, "Less Filling!" Many think teenagers are rebellious, when that is stereotypically only with respect to their parents. However, among their peers, they conform willingly to what social proof tells them is cool and proper.

It's the athlete who says "everyone else is doing steroids so I must in order to compete." It's the insecure, dejected kid who is rejected by the popular straight kids at school and finds acceptance with the wild kids and starts drinking and smoking to fit in. It's the insecure young man who finds "family" and security by joining a street gang. It's the alcohol industry producing television advertisements using young vibrant people who are in the prime of their lives, associating drinking their brand of beer with having fun and attracting the opposite sex, with a message that if you're not drinking alcohol you're not having fun. Social Proof is also at the heart and soul of "Cause Marketing" where the simple sight of an American flag, a "Made in America" label, a "Support Our Troops," sign, and/or affiliating your brand with the "Green" cause of the environment, Aids awareness, breast cancer research, or children's charities, "proves" you and your organization are "socially" responsible and worth associating with.

5. Emphasize Similarity

We like people who are similar to us and are more willing to say yes to their requests. It's the television commercial that interviews ordinary people like us on the street who endorse the product. It's the coach who gets out and runs the two miles with his players whom he has told to run. It's being able to counsel and comfort someone in a tough situation because they know you have experienced exactly what they are going through and can share what you thought and did to handle it, learn from it and move on.

6. Exploit Scarcity

We perceive that limited access to something gives it more value and urgency. "Limited Offer," "One Day Sale," "Once In a Lifetime Opportunity," "Speak Now or Forever Hold Your Peace." It says that every holiday season, parents (Santa Claus) find at least one "must have toy" sold out after they have promised it to their children. And because "Santa knows that they've been good" the children know they will get it! In 1984 it was the Cabbage Patch Kid doll that created the Christmas scramble. Later on, it was the "Furby" doll that was in short supply and out of stock when I went to buy it. To insure it was under the tree on Christmas morning, I spent $500 at an exclusive auction to secure one of these "promised" dolls" that cost only $50 when available in stores.

It's the Church of Jesus Christ of Latter Day Saints (Mormons) building a new Temple in your area and inviting the general public in for an open house so anyone who chooses can take a complete tour before the church dedicates it and closes the doors to non-members. The motivation to take the tour is not because you will see spectacular architecture and art that you can't see in other beautiful religious buildings and European cathedrals. It's that if you don't go in the temple this week, you will never again have the chance. What goes on in Mormon Temples is not "secret," but after they give the dedicatory prayer it becomes "sacred" and only church members in good standing are allowed in.

7. Exemplify Abundance

Scarcity is a positive influencer. However, having a *scarcity mentality* is extremely negative and counter-productive. If we believe success is limited, that there is only "just enough for me" and therefore, I will scratch, kick and claw my way to the top, cheat, steal, step on and over others, and burn bridges to get the small amount of success that is available at the moment, we may have short term results, but in the long haul, we will fail miserably. These are they who have stopped dreaming mighty dreams, risking and growing and working hard on a good, clean, pure, powerful, positive goal; those who are stagnant and out of insecurity, put others down to make themselves feel like they are progressing and better than they are. We must never have a scarcity mentality. We must have an Abundance Mentality.

Where much is given much is expected. The primary purpose in life is to make ourselves better today than we were yesterday, so we are in the required positive emotional state to make everybody else around us better to the degree they say, "I like me best when I'm with you I want to see you again." We must understand that we are *sharing* this world with all living creatures. The only way we will ever avert war, establish world peace, stop global warming, eliminate hunger, cure disease, defeat poverty and create a world in which everybody believes they are here for a reason, is to believe that the same God who made you made me too, and to have an Abundance Mentality toward influence that no matter who you are or where you live, there is enough to go around for all of us!

8. Network

Networking is socializing with a strategic purpose, based on the commitment that we are willing to pay any price and travel any distance to associate with extraordinary human beings." We must also be willing to do whatever is required to "position" our selves in our neighborhoods, circle of friends and communities, so when anyone needs the products and services that we specialize in, they will automatically think of us, come to us, and buy from us. For example, I was playing golf with one of my close friends at a fabulous Country Club in Syracuse, New York. He is CEO of a Fortune 500 company and mingles in a circle of high-roller influential associates. As we left the clubhouse to go to the first tee, a fourth man was put with our group who shared my golf cart.

As we got acquainted throughout the four-hour game, I learned that he had been one of the senior partners in a top international accounting firm. I also learned that he had just moved back to Syracuse – his dream home – and his firm had promised him he would never have to move again. When the corporate office changed its mind and told him he must relocate one more time, he told them to take their job and shove it.

You would think that was rather stupid to walk away from all the seniority, benefits, and security. His friends thought he was foolish. I asked him to explain his strategy.

He said he had joined the Country Club and was going to play golf every day, six days a week, for two full months. And that's just what he did. Almost one year to the day, I was back in Syracuse having dinner at the Country Club with my same CEO friend. As he introduced me to different friends throughout the evening, one man sitting across the room kept staring at me. I asked who he was, and he laughed.

"Do you remember playing golf here last year with John?" He was in your cart. Well, he is now my accountant. In fact, he has one of the largest independent accounting firms in the entire Syracuse, Liverpool and Rome metropolis. Most of my good buddies use him. This country club even uses him. He's a tax wizard. He's terrific!"

Because John understood the only place from which a person can grow is where he or she is, he didn't wait for the customer to come to him. Rather, he went to where the customer was – physically and emotionally. He used the country club membership to pre-qualify his prospects. He wanted wealthy businessmen who needed his in-depth tax knowledge and could afford his specialized service. Then he simply went to where they were and gently invited them to grow.

Because this is true, don't you think we should do something on a daily, weekly, monthly and annual basis to make ourselves more interesting, more informed, more qualified and more accessible so our potential clients and current customers want to be around us, socialize, see us time and time again in various aspects and interests of life, and want to continue to do business with us?

Be More Interesting, More Informed, More Qualified, More Accessible

- **Physically:** Join a health spa and exercise; take lessons until you are good enough to play golf and tennis with anyone;

- **Socially:** Organize a book club or master mind study group; play bridge or Gin as a member of the Country Club; take potential customers shopping and to lunch and dinner at unique places; visit art galleries, swap meets and fairs with someone new each week;

- **Educationally:** Be a life long learner always taking classes in something to broaden your horizons;

- **Spiritually:** Regularly attend a church or synagogue (not out of tradition, but out of conviction) and know the doctrine of your faith; volunteer for charitable causes and serve on their boards;

- **Financially:** Never let your dreams slide down to the level of your income – always bring your income up to the level of your dreams;

- **In Your Community:** Be the very best, most involved parent you can possibly be so other parents and their children look to you for strength and inspiration; volunteer as a youth coach; join civic service clubs like Rotary, Kiwanis, and Junior League; support the Chamber of Commerce and the Boy Scouts of America; always have great season tickets to major sporting events, college games, the Symphony, Ballet, Theater, and attend all "cool" concerts!

Remember, the goal is to be seen as someone very involved and supportive in the community and to make everybody around you better, stimulated and re-energized about living life to the fullest.

SUMMARY

The best way to summarize the practical application of these *Eight Principles and Methods of Significant Influence* is to put them into a single paragraph, about a single theme, sometimes out of order: "Thank you so much for your help. I really appreciate you hooking me up with the right people and resources to accomplish my goal (create value and flow). Do you love music and realize its power?" (the question to start them down your chosen and controlled path). I hope so because I want you to download the *link* I've included here to listen to the special tune that illuminates my thanks to you (reciprocation) for giving me so much of your time and energy.

As you listen it should soothe your soul and remind you (atmosphere) of our wonderful friendship. It's so great to work with someone who thinks like me, enjoys the same things I do, and who has been raised with the same values as I have (similarity). Although some in my industry are not ethical and should be stopped (conscience), everybody in a leadership position in my organization, which you will soon also occupy, has incredible integrity, class and work ethic (leadership), which we will need to keep up with (social proof) if you and I are to remain competitive.

I admire you not just because you are a corporate leader and influencer in our community (authority), but for all you have done and what you stand for (respect) as I appreciate your positive attitude (attitude) as you fit me into (abundance) the only appointment slot you had available all month (scarcity). Thanks. I owe you big time (repeated reciprocation). I can't wait to meet with you and figure out our mutual friends (networking).

And this process of using one or more of these Eight Principles and Methods of Influence continues to recycle itself to perpetuate relationships onward and upward! Bottom line? The Art of Significant Selling, Marketing and Closing More Deals is influencing others to do something they would not normally do, showing them something they cannot see themselves, and taking them to a higher place than they knew existed. The Art of Influence is inspiring others to do what you need them to do while making them believe it is *their* idea. This turns our work into a game, and networking into nothing more than using our influence to help others always leave us saying, 'I like me best when I'm with you, I want to see you again!

CHAPTER SEVENTEEN

THE ART OF GAINING A COMPETITIVE ADVANTAGE BY DOING WHAT YOUR COMPETITION IS NOT WILLING TO DO

"Southwest Airlines has the best customer satisfaction record, based on U.S. Transportation Department statistics, of any airline in America, the fewest complaints filed per 100,000 passengers carried. We are in the 'customer service business' and just happen to be flying people around on airplanes!"

—Herb Kelleher

"We brought prices down, down, down so they are now essentially commodities. So if we want to succeed in this business, we have to move in a direction of adding other value to the relationship with our clients. And so where I might have said 15 years ago, 'We want to be the best discount brokerage,' today I want to be the best 'relationship company' in financial services."

—Charles Schwab

Gaining a 'competitive advantage' in the market place is not gained by doing more than your competition. It is established and maintained by doing what your competition is not willing to do. When we do, and exceed expectations, not only are we creating a memorable, significant customer experience, but in the process we are proving to ourselves that we are valued and needed.

In contemporary American society, we can't afford to wait for someone to tell us or show us that we are needed. It may never happen. We could go for months before we experience this crucial validation. So what do we do – give up, quit, kill ourselves? Most definitely not. Whom are we fooling to think that society has to give our lives meaning, purpose, and excitement? We bear responsibility to do something on a daily basis to prove to ourselves that we are needed.

If you don't feel needed at work, participate more, volunteer, and get involved on committees and event- planning boards. If you don't feel needed at home, participate more, get involved. If you don't feel needed by your children, participate more, get involved in their world, volunteer in their schools, host their parties at your home, stay in touch, get involved in their friends' lives. If you don't feel needed in your neighborhood or world, vote, participate in charity organizations, give more than you take, and leave everything and everyone in better shape than you found them.

The glory of love is not companionship, but rather the spirited inspiration that comes when we discover that someone else believes in us and is willing to trust us. Love is knowing that I don't love you because I need you (this is codependence); I need you because I love you, and I need you to need me, too (this is interdependence). To illustrate the notion of love as the experience of being needed, I offer another story about a death – not just any death, one that really hit home for me.

Dad's Last Day

My dear, sweet dad battled cancer for six and a half years. As the pain mounted and Dad's last day was approaching, I hoped I could be by his bedside when he took his last breath. That didn't happen for me. I had to fly out to Seattle, Washington, to give two speeches to two large groups – one at a conference on Friday morning, the other on Saturday.

I was staying at the Seattle Airport Marriott Hotel. It was early Friday morning, October 12. I had shaved and showered and put on my coat and tie when the phone rang. Thinking it was my ride to the convention center, I picked up the phone and almost flippantly said, "I'll be right there." Fifteen seconds of silence later, my younger brother's voice came through, "Dad passed away this morning at seven a.m."

I sat down on the bed, the tears flowing down my cheeks. "How is Mom?" "Good." "Give her a big hug and a kiss for me, and tell her I'll phone her in a little while." Paul then asked me the gazillion-dollar question, "What are you going to do?" After thinking it over, I said, "I'm going to go make my speech. That's what Dad would want me to do. He always taught us to only make commitments that we can keep and to always keep those commitments."

I couldn't imagine being the meeting planner with more than thirty-five hundred people sitting in the audience and not have the speaker show up. I told my brother that I needed to stay and speak, spend the night, speak the next day, and then hustle home. I hung up and broke down, crying like a baby. My dad, my hero, was gone. I felt wrenched with regrets. Every thought and word was, "I wish I… If only I had…" Yes, I've done a lot of pretty cool things in my life and have had an exciting time. But I would trade all of it for one more day with my dad. When I interview older people, I am often told that they do not have regrets for things they did; they have regrets only for the things they did not do. I know what they mean.

The phone rang again. This time it was my ride. I told him I would be right down. I went into the washroom, splashed water onto my face, left my room, and stepped into the elevator. As the elevator doors closed, the corner of a bellman's cart crammed its way through the narrow opening and the doors reopened. On the elevator came an overzealous, way-too-cheery bellman. He pushed his cart to the middle, forcing me back to the rear corner. Trying to avoid eye contact, I stood with my head down, hands clasped in the "elevator position."

As the doors closed, he blurted, "Whoa! Did you see the beautiful sunshine today? I've lived here in Seattle all of my eighteen years, and it's rained every single day. You must have brought the happy weather with you. How ya doin'?"

Not looking up, I said, "Fine." He kept staring at me until he again blurted, "No, sir, you're not fine. Your eyes are red and a little puffy. You've been crying."

"Yeah. I just found out that my dad died this morning, and I'm really sad."

"Whoa," the bellman said. He went quiet until the doors opened at the lobby. He went left and I went right.

I had to dig deeper that night than I had ever dug to rise to the occasion, but I did, and I made my speech. At the end of my speech, I told the audience I would conclude with a song from one of my albums. I told them I was singing it because my dad had died that morning, and it would be the first time he had ever heard me sing it in public.

I finished the song and had the driver take me back to the Seattle Airport Marriott Hotel. When I walked into the hotel room, I found a basket of fruit resting on the chest of drawers. Not your basic basket delivered from the hotel gift shop with the colored cellophane cover, ribbon bow, and small sterile stamped card from the manager that seldom gets your name right – 'Thanks for staying with us, Ralphie.' This was a broken basket, slightly smashed on one side. It appeared as if it was a last-minute gesture executed with limited resources.

Whoever delivered it was obviously into presentation because the crinkled portion of the basket was turned toward the wall and covered by a big rubberized leaf that had apparently been picked off the fake tree in the lobby. In the basket, I found two oranges, an apple, a big ripe tomato, and a huge carrot. Most important, I found a handwritten note that read:

"Mr. Clark, I'm sure sorry your dad died. I was off work today at 5 p.m., but I came back tonight so I could be here for you. Room service closes at 10 p.m., but the kitchen has decided to stay open all night long so they can be here just for you. If you need anything, just call and ask for me." It was signed, " James – the bellman in the elevator."

James was not the only one to sign the card: Every employee that night at the Seattle Airport Marriott Hotel did. I have it framed and hanging in my office. Here we have James, an eighteen-year-old young man, the youngest and lowest-paid person on the entire employee payroll, who "gets" three things: First, you can't pay enough for experience. (And PS: Age has nothing to do with success or significance. How do we know? Some of the greatest songs you'll ever hear were written by young men and women. Why? Because they have access to the same twelve notes the old folks do.)

Second, James realizes money isn't a motivator; exceeding expectations is. He clearly understands that we are not paid by the hour, but for the value we bring to that hour.

Third, James understands how to create loyalty. Because of his extraordinary covenant to service before self, and his willingness to do what his competition is not willing to do, he endeared me to the Marriott brand and the city of Seattle forever. In fact, every time I speak, I stay at the posh hotel where my clients are holding the meeting. However, because of James, whenever I speak in Seattle, Washington, I always stay at the Airport Marriott Hotel, even if I have to rent a car at my own expense and drive two hours out of my way to get there.

What it's really all about is unconditionally loving and giving more than we take so that we prove to ourselves that we are truly needed. We can do this in our personal lives, but we can also do this at work, with customers and bosses alike, with everyone we meet. Unconditionally loving and giving – not because they have to, but because they expect it of themselves – is what James and his colleagues did so well that night.

Chapter Eighteen

Exceeding Expectations

"Conclusion On A Humorous Note"

On every commercial airline flight we are force-fed the infamous "Pre-Flight Safety Demonstration." But… do you really listen to it? If you do, we need to have a serious chat! Ha! Anyone who has to be taught how to put a seatbelt on should never be allowed in public unsupervised! And the part that irritates me the most is when they tell us to "bring our seats up to the most upright and uncomfortable position." They emphatically believe that an inch and a half will determine if you live or die? I survived a plane crash in 1988 and trust me when I tell you that when you finally hit the ground an inch and a half does not make a difference! There is crap all over the place!! And the flight attendents lie to us when they explain, "we are here for your safety." No. When you are going down they are strapped in and screaming just like we are!!

Because I have flown over six million miles just on Delta Airlines, and have survived a plane crash, just once I wish the flight attendants would give me the microphone to give my version of the pre-flight safety demonstration: "In the event of an emergency a little gold cup is going to konk you on the head. When you stop screaming brace yourself for a 200 feet-per-second vertical dive. And if you are traveling with more than one child, pick your favorite! Because you ain't got time to make another decision!"

What happens when we get on an airplane where the flight attendant is exceeding expectations and delivers the same safety demonstration in an entertaining way that makes flying fun? Or better still, turns the terrible into terrific? Do we not always remember these experiences, seek them out again and again, and encourage our friends and associates to do the same? Oh yea!!

On one Delta flight we were coming in for a landing at the Dallas/ Fort Worth airport, when our jet hit heavy turbulence and bounced all over the sky. When we finally touched down, we hit loud and hard, bounced, hit again, bounced, and hit a third time, this time staying on the ground.

As we taxied to the gate, the flight attendant spoke over the public address system, "Welcome to Dallas, Texas. If you enjoyed your flight, tell your friends you flew Delta Airlines. If you did not enjoy your flight, tell your friends you flew Southwest. And please remain seated with your seat belt fastened tightly while Captain Kangaroo bounces our plane to the terminal."

As we got off the plane, the elderly woman walking in front of me stopped the pilot and asked, "Did we really land, or did we get shot down?"

What are willing to do that no one else is willing to do that makes you and your brand stand out, so we always choose you, and not just somebody who does what you do? Yes, everybody wants to win, but very few are willing to prepare to win. Go for it my friend, and always remember when it comes to Selling, Marketing and Closing More Sales, the "Significant" know It is not enough to say, 'I will do my best.' We must succeed in doing that which is necessary!